HOW TO GET
A MORTGAGE
IN 24 HOURS

HOW TO GET A MORTGAGE IN 24 HOURS

Revised Edition

JAMES E. A. LUMLEY

WILEY

JOHN WILEY & SONS

New York • Chichester • Brisbane • Toronto • Singapore

Library of Congress Cataloging in Publication Data

Lumley, James E. A.
    How to get a mortgage in 24 hours / by James Lumley. — 2nd ed.
      p.   cm.
    Includes bibliographical references.
    ISBN 0-471-51343-1. — ISBN 0-471-51344-X (pbk.)
    1. Mortgage loans—United States.   I. Title.
HG2040.5.U5L85   1990
332.7′2—dc20   89-22737

Printed in the United States of America

10 9 8 7 6 5 4 3 2 1

CONTENTS

1. HOW TO GET YOUR MORTGAGE
   IN 24 HOURS   1

   The Magic of Borrowing Other People's Money, 1
   The Truth about Money Lenders, 4
   The Quickest Way to Get Mortgage Financing for a
      Home or Small Investment, 6
   How to Always Satisfy a Lender in Three Easy Steps:
      Value/Quality of Property; Source of Money to
      Repay Loan; Profitability for a Lender, 8
   Preparing the Surefire Proposal, 10
   How You Can Always Get Your Mortgage, 26
   The Secret of Getting a Quick Mortgage, 28

2. ALL YOU NEED TO KNOW ABOUT
   MORTGAGES   31

   The Basics of Mortgage Financing, 31
   The Big Four: The Four Basic Types of Mortgages, 32
   Innovative Techniques of Creative Financing, 44
   Mortgaging a Home versus an Investment Property,
      46
   How to Decide Whether Short or Long Term Works
      Best for You, 47

What Terms You Should Always Have in a
  Mortgage Agreement, 50
When to Turn to Professionals, 54

3. DECIDING HOW MUCH YOU CAN AFFORD   57

How Much Can You Afford?, 57
Shop for the Best Rates, 58
Private and Public Loan Guidelines, 60
Making the Most of Your Borrowing Power, 62
Adjusting Your Down Payment, 62
The Problem of a Low Down Payment, 63
Mortgage Insurance, 64
How Points Affect Affordability, 64
How Variable Rates Play Havoc with Your Budget, 65

4. CHOOSING THE RIGHT MORTGAGE   69

Shopping for a Mortgage, 70
Compare Loans to Decide Which Is Best, 76
Guidelines for Comparing Loans, 80
Six Points on Choosing a Mortgage, 83

5. WHERE DO YOU GET YOUR MORTGAGE MONEY?   85

Whom Do You Ask for Your Mortgage? From
  Bankers to Sellers, 85
Seven Sources for Money and How to Approach
  Each, 86
How to Select the Best Money Source, 91

6. GETTING CREATIVE WITH CONVENTIONAL FINANCING   95

The First Choice: Do You Want to Gamble on
    Interest Rates?, 95
When the Conventional Loan May Be Best for You, 97
Shopping for the Conventional Loan, 98
Selecting the Best Banker, 99
How to Negotiate Down Payments and Interest Rates, 100
What Do You Do When They Ask for "Points"?, 102
The Benefits of Less Red Tape, 103
Assume the Existing Mortgage, 104
Make Your Own Deal, 106
How to Negotiate the Best Terms, 107
What Your Banker Can and Cannot Do, 109
Inside Tips on Conventional Loans, 110

7. WHAT YOU NEED TO KNOW ABOUT ADJUSTABLE RATE LOANS   113

The Different Kinds of Adjustable Rate Loans, 114
Why They Have Substantially Lower Rates, 120
Less Risk Than You Think, 121
Rates Are Tied to the Money Market, 122
Rate Fluctuation, 122
How to Protect Yourself Against Rising Rates, 123
Advantages and Disadvantages of ARMs, 124
Converting to a Fixed Rate: The Renegotiable
    Mortgage, 125
The Adjustable Balloon Mortgage, 127
Negotiating Manageable Payments, 128
How to Protect Yourself Against the Pitfalls of ARMs, 130

8. WHEN THE SELLER GIVES YOU THE MORTGAGE   133

Help From the Seller: A Two-Way Advantage, 133

Assuming the Seller's Mortgage, 135

The Traditional Second Mortgage, 137

The Wraparound Mortgage and How It Works, 141

When You Want a Bond for Deed, 143

When a Lease with Option Makes Sense, 144

A Variation: Management Agreement with Option (MAO), 148

Exchanging Property, 151

The Easy Way to Sell Yourself to the Seller, 153

How to Avoid the Gamble in Seller Financing, 154

9. WHEN YOU HAVE LITTLE OR NO CASH TO PUT DOWN   157

How to Get Started with No Cash, 158

Buying with No Money Down, 158

When It's Best to Add a Little, 162

Fifteen Ways to Buy with Little or No Cash, 164

The Do's and Don't's of Buying with Little or No Money Down, 173

10. INNOVATIVE TECHNIQUES FOR CREATIVE FINANCING   177

Converting Equity through a Reverse Mortgage, 177

The Price-level Adjusted Mortgage (PLAM), 179

Twenty-five Ways to Finance Any Property, 182

11. HOME EQUITY LOANS 199

Cash in Your Home Secured by a Mortgage, 199
Major Types of Home Equity Loans, 200
Comparing Basic Elements, 201
Deductibility of Home Equity Loans, 206
Keep Bookkeeping in Order, 208
Three Questions You Need to Ask Yourself about
    Applying for a Home Equity Loan, 209
Problems with Borrowing Home Equity Money, 210
Why a Home Equity Loan Is Worth Considering, 211

12. REFINANCING YOUR EXISTING LOAN 215

Saving Money through Refinancing, 215
Renegotiating When It Is to Your Advantage, 216
Targeting the Least Expensive Money, 217
Renegotiating the Best Terms, 219
Discounting the Loan Balance, 219
Costs of Refinancing, 221
Making the Decision, 222
The Best Source for Your Refinancing Needs, 226
Using a Second Mortgage to Restructure Your
    Existing Financing, 227
Interest Deductibility in Refinancing, 228
Four-Point Guideline for Refinancing, 229

13. MORTGAGES KEEP YOUR TAXES DOWN 231

Tax Breaks in Real Estate Financing, 233
Deducting Interest Saves Taxes, 241

Depreciation Cuts Taxable Income, 242
Keeping Track of Your Tax Basis, 244
When to Negotiate a Tax-Deferred Exchange, 246
The Installment Sale Tax Break, 250
Pyramiding Your Wealth Without Paying Taxes, 250
Choosing a Knowledgeable Accountant, 252

14. WHY FINANCING IS THE KEY TO BIG PROFITS   253

Mortgages Give You the Money to Make Money, 253
Mortgages Are the Key to Real Estate Success, 254
Borrowing Your Way to Riches, 255
Mortgages Are the Quickest Way to Great Wealth, 256
Negotiation Requires Preparation, 259
You Can Do It All in Your Spare Time, 260
The Power of Using Other People's Money, 260
Smart Mortgage Financing Can Give You an Income
    for Life, 261
How to Spend the Thousands of Dollars You've Saved
    by Reading This Book, 263

Index, 265

PREFACE

How to Get a Mortgage in 24 Hours is in its second edition, and its principle of helping you find low-cost financing in the quickest possible time is even more relevant today. Many new alternative mortgage plans are analyzed in this book, and new guidelines are given that will help you choose among these competing alternatives, all with the goal of saving you money. Thorough discussions are given on how loans work, how to evaluate what they cost, and how to choose what is best for you.

We are a nation of movers. Each year residential transfers increase almost 10 percent over the previous year. One reason is relatively stable interest rates on property loans. As rates fall it becomes easier to sell one house to buy another. Today, mortgage rates are less than they were on properties financed in the early 1980s.

The foreseeable future bodes well for the continuation of these modest rates as well as substantial quantities of mortgage money being available.

It seems that all we need to do to get on this bandwagon of money is to ask, and in part this is true. However, it is not as easy as it sounds. Banks have so many requests for mortgage money that they often tend to be arbitrary and overly selective of those to whom they lend these funds. Also, time is often critical in securing a mortgage commitment. In this book you will see how to find shortcuts through this selection process and thus guarantee your getting a mortgage in the quickest amount of time, whether you get your financing from a banker or a seller.

Is it possible to get a mortgage in 24 hours? Yes—if you are willing to spend time and energy paving the way for that one-day commitment. This means you will have to choose your lender with care, prepare a convincing presentation of your case, and make allowance ahead of time for certain procedures that are beyond your control.

What are some of the procedures that can delay the mortgage commitment? The irregular or overloaded meeting schedule of a bank's mortgage committee is often one of the slow-down points. A second bottleneck is the current shortage of real estate appraisers; in busy buying times in recent years lenders sometimes have had to wait as long as 45 to 120 days for appraisals to come through. The present shortage of real estate attorneys causes still another delay. And a fourth slow-down point has been the backlog of credit reports. A few years ago, a bank could expect a credit check to take one to three days; that same report today often takes more than a month.

As a home buyer who wants a mortgage and wants it now, you will have to anticipate these delays and circumvent them by doing much of the legwork, planning, and information-gathering ahead of time. This book will tell you how to go about those tasks in order to speed up the lending process.

In your quest for a quick mortgage, you will probably find lenders willing to cooperate, because many banks are growing increasingly aggressive in their pursuit of reliable borrowers. The current competition among lenders has forced them to be more responsive to the needs of consumers, and they are learning to move more quickly.

Some large banks are even promising homebuyers mortgage commitments within minutes. These near-instant loan commitments require only pertinent information on you and the property, but like all loans secured by real estate, they require a satisfactory appraisal, which in many cases may be done that day.

Most banks, and inevitably the one that offers you the best loan, cannot offer instant gratification, but to remain competitive they have in recent years greatly speeded up their paperwork. The key is information; it takes the correct facts—particularly employment verification and appraisal—for the bank to move quickly.

In fact, your job is to jump in there, hustle up the necessary paperwork, and demonstrate to the lender that you are qualified to get that mortgage—and get it "now."

Often nowadays you can be assured of a mortgage even before you find the property. To ensure this quick service, satisfy the lender on three basic points: first, the property value; second, your ability to repay; and third, the profitability of a mortgage for the lender.

You will learn how to make a mortgage proposal satisfying the lender on these points. Professional investors have used such proposals for years, and now you can use them to short-circuit or speed up the bank's appraisal and credit processes. The proposal is easy to prepare—no longer than a few pages showing your banker you are a sound, rational borrower who understands the financial aspects of a mortgage and the bank's need for profit. It convinces the lender that you are familiar with the loan process and that you are a good risk for a loan.

No matter what the loan conditions are in your area, the proposal and accompanying advice for negotiating interest rate and terms found in this book will not only help you get the funds you need in the shortest amount of time, but will save you thousands of dollars. The proposal is the best way to ensure your getting the best deal for the money you need.

Unlike other books on mortgages, this book is not a technical rendition on financial or accounting techniques. In fact, only a few charts show how the basic mortgage works. What it is is a thorough discussion of the many mortgages available and of strategies for negotiating the best one in the shortest amount of time and at the lowest possible cost. It will not make you a financial wizard, but if you read it, you will be able to walk into a bank and talk to a mortgage officer on equal terms.

I am not a banker, but my experience as a real estate broker and my own purchasing and financing of investment property have given me insight into what is necessary for success in getting a rapid and favorable commitment on a mortgage.

This book is easy to understand, even when it explains a specific problem of loan payoff or term negotiation. It gives you step-by-step, surefire methods to achieve success.

The book explains how the different types of mortgages work—from conventional loans to adjustable rate mortgages to creative financing with sellers. It gives you the information you need to make intelligent decisions. It doesn't assume you have any experience with banks or mortgages, but leads you through the basics of what mortgages are all about, how they work, and how to select the right one for you.

The information does not get more detailed with each chapter. If you are familiar with conventional mortgages, you can skip that section and proceed to the section on seller financing. Or perhaps you want to compare conventional and adjustable rate loans, so you skip the explanations of how each one works.

The material in this book will challenge you. It will make you think about the different ways to construct a mortgage with either a bank or a seller and how its terms might be negotiated to benefit you most.

Be wary of the many different formats offered by lending institutions; practically all mortgage alternatives are simply variants of the basic fixed rate conventional loan and the adjustable rate mortgage. Obtaining a mortgage is probably the most complex financial transaction you will make, but with a little wise comparison shopping, you will find the right mortgage no matter what type.

In Chapter 1 you will learn how to construct a mortgage proposal for financing any property in any market in the quickest amount of time. Chapter 2 explains the common types of mortgages. Chapter 3 helps you decide how much money you can comfortably afford to borrow. And Chapter 4 shows you how to choose from the wide variety of loan formats available.

Chapter 5 gives numerous sources for mortgage money and explains how to approach each. Chapter 6 explains conventional financing and how to negotiate the lowest possible interest rate and most advantageous terms. In Chapter 7 the advantages and disadvantages of adjustable rate mortgages are discussed, as well as how to negotiate them and how to protect yourself against their pitfalls. Chapter 8 explores the many aspects of creative financing that can be negotiated with sellers.

In Chapter 9 you will learn about getting a mortgage when you have little or no cash to put down. Chapter 10 gives you inside information on many additional techniques for financing a property. Chapter 11 discusses home equity loans and how they can help you tap your present equity. And Chapter 12, on refinancing, shows you how to acquire cash or consolidate existing loans.

In Chapter 13 you will learn how taxes affect the financing and ownership of real estate, specifically how the current tax law makes financing property one of the best investment techniques you will ever use. Finally, Chapter 14 shows you how to use Other People's Money (OPM) to gain an income for life or, in many cases, great wealth.

This book is not on how to make millions in the real estate business. To be sure, you may end up making a fortune—not only does real estate have the potential to appreciate over the long term, but the interest you pay on the money you borrow is deductible. This makes borrowing money to buy real estate one of the most valuable financial opportunities you have as a homebuyer, but only if you know how to negotiate the best mortgage at the most advantageous cost and terms, and get the lender's commitment in the shortest possible time.

You will want to pay special attention to the many "Key Points" and "Caution Notes" throughout the book. Key Points are fundamental truths—the do's of getting a mortgage. They offer positive solutions. Caution Notes are the don't's; they point out obvious, and sometimes not so obvious, procedures to avoid.

Pay attention to both the problems and the solutions. With honesty and perseverance you will get the right mortgage in the shortest amount of time, ensuring your financial success in real estate.

JAMES E. A. LUMLEY

Amherst, Massachusetts
Spring 1990

HOW TO GET YOUR MORTGAGE IN 24 HOURS 1

THE MAGIC OF BORROWING OTHER PEOPLE'S MONEY

In the not-too-distant past buyers seeking real estate, particularly older people, thought the best way to buy property was with all cash. In fact, many people had this attitude into the 1960s. The times began to take a dramatic turnabout in the early 1970s when the annual inflation rate edged over 4%, then an astronomically high figure. The value of money dropped accordingly. Paying all cash became a foolhardy way to purchase a property. Today, many believe it would be downright stupid. We automatically think of getting a mortgage when we buy real estate.

But getting a mortgage hasn't just been popular in the last decade. Our parents and often our grandparents had financial help, even though minimal by our standards, in the form of a mortgage when they bought real estate.

■ *KEY POINT: Some form of mortgage financing has always been available.*

In the past century millions of people have found security in buying a home or investment property by using other people's

1

money in the form of a mortgage. In fact, today, it is often considered smart to put down little of your own money or no cash at all. Not that full financing is always desirable in purchasing property. If banks know an owner has little equity in a property, thereby making it easy for him to walk away, they are less likely to grant a loan. And banks never want to foreclose, even if an owner encounters difficulty.

Let's consider what a mortgage is. First of all, a mortgage, whether given by a bank, former owner of a property, or even a third party, is a legal, secured instrument on a piece of real estate. It is a negotiation of an amount of money from either a bank or private party, which will in turn be payed on regular installments, generally monthly, by the new borrower of the money, that is, purchaser of the property.

■ *KEY POINT: A mortgage is a negotiated loan secured by a property and paid back in installments.*

Where does this money come from? The most popular source of money in buying a home or investment property in the United States is a bank. A mortgage bank or savings and loan or some other government-insured institution is legally chartered to dispense funds to buyers of property and in turn hold a secured instrument in that property until said mortgage is paid in full. Now, a key point about mortgages. Is it the bank's money? No, generally not. The money lent to the borrower is often money that is either in the bank due to savings-accounts deposits or is borrowed outright from other larger banks, which in turn is also from savings, investors, and other sources.

■ *KEY POINT: Banks lend other people's money.*

What is the mortgage bank's motivation in doing this? The bank gains this pool of funds from their depositors. For example, these small investors invest small amounts of money, perhaps 5–8%, and in turn the bank takes this conglomeration of funds and re-lends it out in the form of mortgages at rates anywhere between 10 and 20%.

If it seems banks make a lot of money on the mortgage you may hold with them, they do. And in this book you will find many tactics for negotiating to get the most advantageous mortgage and lowest interest rate, thereby keeping the bank's profit more reasonable.

■ *CAUTION NOTE:* *Banks make considerable money on interest they charge you.*

If you are buying a house or an investment property, a mortgage is probably critical for you to make the purchase. The most important thing in finding and making the deal, even more important than the property itself, is how you will finance it. There are numerous choices. The bank, as we have mentioned, is one. The other type of mortgage is from a seller. New and interesting techniques to borrow from a bank or seller will be discussed in the following chapters.

■ *KEY POINT:* *Choosing between available financing is the biggest decision in buying.*

Often your home is the best investment you will ever make. Surprising increases in value over relatively short periods of time, sometimes only a few years, make recent home purchases outstanding investments. You also may wish to purchase a summer or vacation home. Here again, the use of borrowed money can make you rich. In real estate investment itself, such as in a rented duplex or larger apartment building, even if owned with other investors, the financing you arrange is critical in determining how much money you will make. So here we will learn how to negotiate the right amount and type of financing.

■ *KEY POINT: Borrowing money is the key to becoming rich.*

Real estate, then, is a business of borrowing money. It is the use of Other People's Money (OPM) to secure a tangible asset, that is, real estate, which in turn will be lived in by you or rented out and grow in value. At the same time, you can enjoy substantial tax savings.

■ *KEY POINT: Real estate is a vehicle for borrowing money.*

Other People's Money is the magic we use to ensure our own financial security. The mortgage allows you to finance the house you live in or an income-producing building. It allows you to pay the cost of this mortgage from money you earn from your regular employment or out of the rental income from the investment itself. The mortgage allows you to acquire ownership of relatively expensive property by putting down only a fraction of cash on the total purchase price.

■ *KEY POINT: A mortgage allows larger purchase than you could make yourself.*

In fact, as we will see in this book ways to borrow as much money as you need to buy a home or income property with a minimum down payment. The use of other people's money is the key to home ownership and investment success.

THE TRUTH ABOUT MONEY LENDERS

Two important things must be understood about mortgage lenders. The first is that they never, never want to foreclose. Once they have lent the money it is extremely important to them that they have made the right decision; never except under the worst of circumstances do they want to take back the property, even if payments are not being made on the loan and it appears that the loan might be in default.

■ *KEY POINT:* *Lenders never want to foreclose.*

The lender is always open to the possibility of extended payments, refinancing, or almost anything that will avoid the decision to foreclose. Foreclosure to them means that they have failed. They have neglected to realize the problem in that particular loan. They are in the business of lending money which in turn makes them a profit. They are not in the business of managing property, particularly property that must be resold, often difficult for an institution, and time-consuming to foreclose.

■ *KEY POINT:* *Banks almost always allow refinancing or extended payments.*

When you're getting a mortgage a strong motivation for the lender is money; they want to make a profit. This leads us to the second and most important thing about mortgage lenders. They want to loan you money. They must lend you money, and as long as in their mind you will satisfy certain minimum financial requirements, they will quickly assent to loaning you money.

■ *KEY POINT:* *Lenders exist to lend you money.*

You may have heard of friends who, in approaching a bank, were turned off by a standoffish mortgage officer who put before them the complicated rigmarole of paperwork which made the process exasperating. This may have even happened to you.

■ *CAUTION NOTE:* *Bankers and paperwork inhibit the loan process.*

The key to getting a mortgage is to understand that the banks must, under reasonable guidelines, lend out their money. If they don't lend it to you, they don't make the profits they're required to do in order to pay back their depositors or those from whom they have borrowed the money they re-lent to you.

In this book we will see guidelines that describe how you can meet the requirements for getting mortgage money.

THE QUICKEST WAY TO GET MORTGAGE FINANCING FOR A HOME OR SMALL INVESTMENT

Time is usually of the essence in getting a mortgage loan. Shopping with your local real estate agent or on your own, you may have found the house you want. You may have even agreed with the seller on price and have signed a purchase agreement.

You may have agreed to take over the property in so many days if you meet certain conditions, such as your ability to obtain financing from a local lending institution. Typically, even though you may not be taking over the property for another month, you are given a limited amount of time, usually five to ten days, in which to secure from a mortgage lender a commitment that you will obtain mortgage funds when the deed is passed from seller to buyer.

■ *KEY POINT:*　*Sales are often conditional upon financing.*

In fact, in this "deposit-taken" stage of a pending sale real estate brokers often don't take the property off the market. Even if you have arranged to purchase a house at full price and have signed a purchase agreement with the seller, the property is held by the brokers in a state of limbo. It means there is a potential sale to you but that it might fall through should there be any problems with financing. Generally there is not, but often brokers will show your intended property, explaining to a second buyer that you, as the first buyer, have the right of first refusal because your sale is conditional upon financing.

■ *CAUTION NOTE: Sales can fall through without a financing commitment.*

This need not be a worrisome problem. In most cases, financing is usually approved for the first buyer and the sale goes through. However, it is critical to ensure on your behalf that there are no slipups in your getting a mortgage commitment. The question then becomes "what is the quickest way for us to arrange financing?" The answer is simply this: All mortgage lenders have a short list of principles that must be satisfied before the bank gives out any mortgage money.

■ *CAUTION NOTE: Bank rules must be satisfied before loan approval.*

These questions are not complicated. You will see with a little preliminary work that they're easy to solve. Here we will take the mystery out of getting the mortgage in the shortest amount of time.

You can get a mortgage in 24 hours—approval on your loan request the day after your initial presentation to the bank. This is not unusual. Real estate brokers and developers, as well as those who have mortgages, do this all the time.

■ *KEY POINT: One-day loans are easy to get.*

What you are going to learn here is some of their time-tested secrets on how they do it; specifically, what you need to do to get a loan. It may seem like a great mystery. It is not. But by no means can a mortgage be obtained by an easy gimmick. By following several simple procedures, you can ensure that 99% of the time you will get the mortgage of your choice in 24 hours,

■ *KEY POINT: Getting a loan is not a mystery.*

Often, for technical reasons, it might take a couple of days for some banks to meet on your loan application; some loan committees in small banks do not meet daily. But even in this situation the bank's loan officer will almost always assure you that you have met the bank's criteria. In big banks that have large pools of mortgage funds to lend out, mortgage decisions are often made daily—all you need to do is be prepared with the right information required by the bank to make its decision.

■ *KEY POINT: Preparation is the key to getting a favorable mortgage commitment quickly.*

HOW TO ALWAYS SATISFY A LENDER IN THREE EASY STEPS: VALUE/QUALITY OF PROPERTY; SOURCE OF MONEY TO REPAY LOAN; PROFITABILITY FOR A LENDER

When lenders make loans, they must make three important decisions. The first is the quality of the property: is the property worth what you have agreed to pay to the seller? Generally, this is not the problem. You would purchase property in the open market, probably in competition with other buyers. Before you reached the bank you may even have negotiated the selling price down from its original asking price. It seems right to you, but occasionally a bank's decision can be delayed by a nasty little procedure called the appraisal process.

■ *KEY POINT:* *The first criterion of the bank: value of property.*

■ *CAUTION NOTE:* *The appraisal process takes time.*

Banks send either their investment committee, made up of their own loan officers, or an appraiser. These people do nothing but ascertain the value of property. Either the committee or the appraiser can make mistakes. Even the staff appraiser, who sees dozen of properties each day, and perhaps a hundred or more weekly, is prone to mistakes. It is understood that the appraiser must occasionally ax a few property values.

Appraisals done by in-house staff are not as thoroughly researched or as detailed as those you would get from an independent appraiser. Bank appraisals are generally quick, one-page studies based primarily on the square footage of the building and its age. These "quicky" appraisals often do not consider such tangible values as the neighborhood in which the house is located or its style or antique value.

■ *CAUTION NOTE:* *Staff appraisers are prone to mistakes.*

What you will learn here is how to short-circuit or "support" this appraisal process.

The second financial criterion critical in satisfying a bank is the source of money to repay the mortgage loan. Here you and your spouse's employment income and any other income you may have from investments or non-job-related sources that can help meet monthly loan payments are stated. This disclosure also takes into account where you stand in the overall financial picture, including your current assets and liabilities and income and expenses. This is the second requirement of the bank that you can prepare for.

■ *KEY POINT: Satisfy the bank with detailed disclosure of your finances.*

The third and most important criterion the bank makes in deciding a loan is whether it will be profitable for them. This may seem obvious but it is not. All internal decisions by a bank and any mortgage application take this into account.

The interest rate on your mortgage fluctuates with the cost of money in the overall marketplace. It affects the decisions by any particular bank on what interest rate and other costs they charge.

■ *KEY POINT: The loan must be profitable for the bank.*

There's a cost of money and if the bank doesn't get their return on what they charge you they will have a difficult time paying back their depositors or the larger money pools from which they initially borrowed the money.

Let's see what each of these three principles mean in practice and what you can do to ensure your bank will give you a favorable decision in the quickest amount of time.

PREPARING THE SUREFIRE PROPOSAL

The following is one of the simplest and most practical ways to ensure mortgaging financing. Professionals have used it for years. Whether you are buying a small apartment building, huge shopping center, or, as in most cases, a family home, you can put into a short, three-to-six page proposal, your request for a loan; following the three steps named above, you will almost always be assured of gaining a quick, favorable decision on your request.

■ *KEY POINT: A brief proposal ensures favorable commitment quickly.*

This proposal addresses the internal decisions made by any bank in an objective, nonthreatening way. It provides them with information that they would otherwise have to gain on their own in an often time-consuming process of investigation. In the proposal you will prepare, you must put down the information they need.

There's also an intangible plus in that this proposal, besides providing the pertinent information on which the bank can honor your request, shows the bank that you are a competent businessperson, someone with whom they would like to do business.

■ **KEY POINT:** *A bank is most likely to make a rapid, favorable decision with detailed property information.*

This intangible aspect addresses an important side of the mortgage decision, the unstated side that most bankers rarely talk about. The business of loaning money is not purely technical; it's partly emotional. You are not presenting a loan request to a computer. From the loan officer to the investment committee to the appraiser, bankers are living, emotional people. Part of how they make their decision is based on an emotional, intangible need beyond the technical reasons to make or not make the loan, almost for reasons that are undefinable.

■ **CAUTION NOTE:** *Banks often make emotional, nontechnical decisions.*

This proposal helps reduce any intangible need not to grant your loan. The proposal gives you added protection, eliminating as much as possible the extraneous or nontechnical reasons for not getting the loan. You will know that if you do not get the loan, it will be because your $10,000 income without any savings doesn't support a $250,000 house loan, or the half-million dollar house to hold you and the nine kids is located in a neighborhood of $35,000 dilapidated shacks.

■ *KEY POINT:*   *A mortgage proposal ensures reasonable success.*

Let's look closely at what each of the major parts of this proposal entails.

Jumping the Gun on the Appraisal

First we address the problem of value or quality of the property. You are not going to pretend to be a qualified appraiser, but you can, in a professional way, follow some of the principles that appraisers use. In fact, with minimal research, you can often do a more thorough job than the bank appraiser.

■ *KEY POINT:*   *Provide the bank with a mini-appraisal.*

The most important criterion in determining value of a property is how the negotiated price of the property you wish to buy compares with properties comparable in size, neighborhood, and amenities that have recently sold.

This is not difficult for you to do. If you are going through a real estate broker in buying a property, he or she can help you with information on comparable sales. If you don't have a broker, the job is just as easy. Most real estate offices keep specific information on sold properties and are often glad to share it with you. All you need to do is pick out from their "sold" file properties of similar size and compare them against your property (eg, number of bedrooms and baths, dining room, study, living room, kitchen, one- or two-car garage, rather specific amenities such as extra land area, swimming pool, or even gazebo). You want a sale within the last year, preferably the last six months, that will as closely as possible duplicate the house or income property you wish to purchase.

■ *KEY POINT:* *Comparable sales verify value.*

Another criterion is the general economic level of the neighborhood in which your subject house is located. The following chart is intended as a sample for you to follow in gaining two or three comparable prices of properties listing what they contain, their selling price, and exactly when they sold.

Photographs of the property will help but are not essential.

COMPARABLE VALUE ANALYSIS					
	Property #1		Property #2		Property #3
Address	65 Armister		34 Weems		9 Bruiet
Date of sale	January 1985		June 1985		May 1985
Sale Price		$91,500		$89,500		$81,500
Adjustments	(−)	(+)	(−)	(+)	(−)	(+)
Adjustment for Date	0	$1,500	0	0	0	0
Age/condition	0	0	0	0	0	$3,500
Size/utility	$6,000	0	0	0	$3,000	0
Kitchen/bath	$1,200	0	0	0	$1,200	0
Porch/garage	0	0	0	$1,500	0	$2,000
Site/location	$2,500	0	$2,500	0	0	0
Other/amenity	0	$1,200	0	$1,200	0	$1,200
Subtotals	$8,200	$94,200	$2,500	$94,200	$4,200	$88,200
Adjustment Totals	$86,000		$89,700		$84,000	

Comparable value shown by market = $86,500

Note: Properties similar to property being financed are listed and adjusted to match subject property as closely as possible. Adjusted values are then averaged to show rough value. In this way, what you pay for a property is supported by common-sense facts such as selling prices, and size and location adjustments in the marketplace. No matter how large the property, this appriasal technique can be used to justify value.

Figure 1.1. Chart on comparable properties.

Note that a professional appraiser adds and subtracts specific dollar amounts to make the comparable houses exactly equal to the subject house. You are not going to match prices exactly, you are simply giving the bank information on several previously sold properties that are comparable in physical characteristics to the property you wish to buy. This comparison, more than anything, can justify the price that you have agreed to pay for your property. It is invaluable information in guiding your bank to affirm the value of the property you wish to buy. Too often, conservative bankers will turn down a loan because they just don't have this information to go on.

■ *CAUTION NOTE: Use selling prices only.*

In picking out properties that match yours, don't choose similar sale prices. Look for properties that are comparable in nature (physical condition, neighborhood, and sold under a similar economic climate) and then, and only then, hopefully those selling prices will put your property in a favorable light.

If these properties have all sold in the last six months, the current market should be similar to that under which they sold.

You will find that this mini-appraisal, based on easy information you can get from local real estate agents or even a salesperson with whom you may be doing business, will go a long way in leading to a favorable decision by the bank, since the value of the property is often the key factor in the mortgage lender's decision.

■ *KEY POINT: Property value is the most important criterion in granting a loan.*

Your Own Financial Profile

The second major part of this proposal is a one-page outline of your assets and your income. It's nothing more than a quick financial profile of yourself that goes a long way to speeding up the mortgage process.

This financial part of the proposal is easy to prepare. The sample here is basic but includes all major categories that will be needed. On the first half of the page will be your balance sheet, specifically listing your assets and liabilities, which you can see equal each other. On the second half will be your income and expense statement detailing annual earnings and costs.

Let's understand something about your financial situation. You don't have to be worth a fortune to get a mortgage loan. You don't even need a long history of annual income, nor do you need to make a huge salary. You need to make enough money to afford payments if the property is your home, perhaps less if rental income will more than cover these payments.

PERSONAL FINANCIAL PROFILE

Income Statement:

Employment earnings (husband and wife)	$27,000
Extra services income	$4,500
Interest income	$1,100
Net rental income	$3,100
Other income	0
Total annual income	*$35,700*

Expense Statement:

Rent	$10,800
Utilities	$3,800
Telephone	$700
Babysitter	$800
Food	$4,500
Car	$2,400

(Continued)

Figure 1.2. Personal asset and liability and income and expense chart.

Educational expenses	$1,250
Insurance	$2,000
Loans	$4,000
Travel	$2,500
Miscellaneous	$1,000
Total annual expenses	*$33,750*

BALANCE SHEET

Assets:

Cash in checking accounts	$1,100
Cash in savings account	$2,300
Money due	$800
Loans owed by others	$1,500
Stock owned	$4,500
Value of life insurance	$300
Real estate owned	0
Cars	$6,500
Personal property	$3,500
Other assets	$1,300
Total assets	*$21,800*

Liabilities:

Accounts payable	$1,100
Notes payable	$9,500
Income taxes	$1,300
Mortgages	0
Other debts	$800
Total liabilities	*$12,700*
Net worth (assets minus liabilities)	*$9,100*

Figure 1.2 (*Continued*)

■ *KEY POINT: Wealth and large income are important but not critical.*

Some lenders today even look approvingly at upwards of 50% of your total income going toward mortgage payments.

Even if you are buying an apartment building or a commercial block for hundreds of thousands of dollars, your income is often less important than purchasing the house, since the actual income from the apartments or commercial tenants is what will pay the loan.

■ *KEY POINT:* *Rental income of an investment property pays the mortgage.*

If you're married, make sure that both you and your spouse's earnings are listed. Lenders accept the total annual income of both spouses. Just detail this information separately to show the source of each.

Your wages may come from a variety of sources. Some of it may come from a direct hourly or annual wage. Some may come from extra self-employment such as consulting or making furniture. The point is to list every source of income. Interest from savings accounts, the capital of which is listed under your assets, should be included in the income section. Unemployed persons have gotten mortgages based solely on income coming from a trust fund.

■ *KEY POINT:* *Your income can come from different sources.*

All a bank wants is to be assured that the monthly payments are going to be met. It comes back to one of the truths about small bankers. They don't want to foreclose. If they are reasonably satisfied that you have a way to meet the mortgage payments, even it if may be a big sock out of your income, they are likely to grant you the loan.

People often worry about their credit. This worry is largely overdone. Even if you've had credit problems in the past, your present economic situation is more important. The loan is made today under current economic conditions. Most mortgage lenders are called "equity lenders," that is, they're more concerned that the security of their loan be in the value of the property. Your ability to pay the loan is still important but secondary to the bank's overall exposure of funds in the real estate itself. That's why ascertaining the value of the property is more critical than great reserves on your financial statement.

■ *KEY POINT: Credit is not as important as the value of the property.*

However, the financial statement must always be addressed and the most painless way is to include the information as part of your proposal. Don't wait for them to ask you. Giving this information up front, even if it's not all good, will go a long way to gaining credibility with the bank.

■ *KEY POINT: Personal financial information gains credibility with a bank.*

If you've got lots of assets and make great income in relation to the mortgage you're requesting, that's fine, but if not, realize that it is not the most important criterion on which a mortgage decision is based, and you are going a long way by addressing it truthfully in the proposal.

In fact, banks have less loan trouble with customers who have small amounts of income from a variety of sources than from those with income from a single source that might be lost if the person loses their job. Several-source incomes show the customer is willing to work at a variety of tasks to pay obligations.

■ *KEY POINT: Banks like multiple sources of income.*

So don't try and outguess the bank. Put down your assets and your income truthfully. As long as you, or the property, can reasonably meet payments, you are not likely to be turned down for a loan.

■ *KEY POINT: Banks look for ability to meet payments.*

Making Sure the Lender Gets His Share

At this point in your proposal you have addressed two major criteria that lenders look at closely: the property and the borrower. The last consideration, the lender's profit, may seem to be out of your control, and to some degree it is.

What you need to know is that once you pass the first two criteria you still may not get a mortgage if the bank is not going to make money from the loan.

■ *CAUTION NOTE: Banks must ensure their profit.*

Their profit may seem automatic. After all, they charge you a lot of interest, don't they? Yes, but they must compete with other banks to give you the best deal they can. The answer to this dilemma comes in negotiating a specific loan and mortgage terms.

The loan you request, whether it be a conventional loan, adjustable rate mortgage, variable payment loan, or some other mortgage instrument, combined with the particular interest rate and length of time under which the loan will be paid back, all are factors in whether the bank can make a fair profit—as well as giving you a fair deal.

■ *KEY POINT: Banks profit from a variety of factors: interest rate, length of loan, service fees, and prepayment stipulations.*

This does not mean that you need to offer the bank more interest than they would expect. Generally, banks have stated interest rates for various types of loans. These rates may change weekly, either falling or rising depending on the economic climate.

To negotiate a mutually advantageous loan, you need to be aware of the many different kinds of mortgage instruments and terms that can be negotiated with each bank. Much of this follows in the rest of this book. Armed with knowledge of what mortgages are all about is the best way for you to ensure that you can construct a fair deal—a profitable deal for the bank as well as one that is advantageous for you.

■ *CAUTION NOTE:* *Central to negotiating is knowing the types of* *mortgages available.*

And as you will see in the succeeding chapters, there are many ways to construct a loan. No longer are mortgages just the traditional kind, where interest rate and term were fixed and nonnegotiable. Adjustable rate mortgages, variable payments mortgages, blanket mortgages, trust deeds, and many variations of those are some of the numerous types of instruments that can be negotiated with mortgage lenders.

■ *KEY POINT:* *There are a variety of loans available.*

Not every lender subscribes to every kind of mortgage. Your task is to find out the different possibilities that exist within a particular bank and make a particular request within that framework. A sample loan request is included here.

This request should ensure fairness for both you and the

LOAN REQUEST

I wish to request an 80% mortgage loan of $93,000 at an interest rate of 11½% for a term of 25 years. I understand from preliminary discussions with you that if I pay two percentage points at the closing you will reduce your customary rate of 12¼% to the 11½%. I also request that your prepayment penalty of 3% of the loan balance paid to the bank at the time of sale be reduced to 1½% after 3 years and no fee will be charged after ownership of six years.

Figure 1.3. Sample loan request.

bank. Your concern for the bank's reasonable profitability is one of the best ways for you to gain loan approval.

■ *KEY POINT: Concern for the bank's profitability helps gain a favorable loan commitment.*

Selling Yourself to Your Banker

The final step in your proposal is to write a short cover letter. This need be nothing more than a short description of how much money you will need and what you intend to buy. You could also mention any extenuating circumstances, such as work to be done with the property and how much it might cost. Like the other parts of our proposal, this cover letter should be easily read and understood by the bank. It should be also easy for you to write. The cover letter helps establish you are a responsible person with whom the bank can do business.

■ *KEY POINT: The cover letter capsulizes three points: value, finances and profitability.*

The letter can also refer to the three major parts of the proposal. It should be written in simple terms, short, with its request clear and simply stated.

The cover letter should never be more than one page. It is not the place for you to ramble on about extraneous details for why you need this money so desperately. Business writing should be short and sweet. This letter is not the place for extensive prose. Use short simple words. Stay away from long descriptions. Remember, the purpose of this proposal is to boil down a major financial undertaking into a simple, easy-to-understand request.

■ *KEY POINT: Write a brief statement in clear English.*

COVER LETTER

Mr. Michael Sigafoos, Mortgage Officer
American National Mortgage
New York, Chicago, Miami, Los Angeles

Dear Mr. Sigafoos,

I thank you for the time you have shared with me explaining your loan policy and the different types of mortgages available. At this time I would like to follow up on our talks with a formal proposal for a mortgage.

I have placed a deposit on a single family residence in Heritage Estates in neighboring Winston. The owner and I have agreed to a selling price of $86,500. I intend to put 20% of the purchase down in cash; $12,000 of my own funds will be added to the $5,300 I am borrowing from my family. I would like to borrow $69,200 for a 25-year term.

Enclosed I include recent selling prices for property similar to the one I'm buying. Considering I'm buying several months after these other properties have been sold, I believe I'm getting excellent value and will provide the bank with ample security.

I also enclose a detailed record of my income and expenses and a full disclosure of my assets and liabilities. I believe I can easily meet the needs of monthly payments on this mortgage.

I do hope you will act favorably on this request.

Sincerely,

Figure 1.4. Cover letter.

Your banker does not need to take a long time to make a decision. Usually, favorable decisions are granted almost immediately. Doubtful decisions take more time. The purpose of the proposal is to tip the balance in your favor. It is a logical presentation of factual information, which is the best way to sell yourself to your banker.

■ *KEY POINT: A well-constructed proposal is likely to tip the mortgage decision in your favor.*

Convincing the Homeowner

This book is not only on getting loans from institutional lenders. It is also about negotiating a loan with the person from whom you are purchasing the property. In this case a different proposal is to be used. Here you do not need to convince the seller of the value of his property in comparison with other recent sales, but often it's helpful to you to give him or her an understanding of your financial position. In this way you show the seller your ability to meet payments.

■ *KEY POINT: The proposal to the seller need not contain appraisal information.*

You can also outline the different terms with which the loan might be constructed, showing how they might be of benefit to the seller and how he or she may profit.

Your request for the seller to take back a mortgage is two-part. The first part demonstrates your financial stability, and the second the benefits he or she will derive on the holding of this loan.

A sample letter is contained herein to give you an idea as to how best to sell a seller. Note that this is a place where you can be less objective than you needed to be with your banker. You don't need to be as detailed on your assets and liabilities and income and expenses. You only need to show in a general way nothing more than what they might need to know, perhaps offering more information if your proposal is accepted.

■ *KEY POINT: The letter to the seller is more flexible.*

In this letter you might mention what kind of mortgage you would like to negotiate, the interest rate, and such terms that might be of advantage to both parties, or particularly, those that might entice the seller. Perhaps you could pay off a large portion of the loan at a date sooner than the full term of the loan. Perhaps you could bring out details of the amount of interest that is paid over the term of the mortgage. The interest is usually a considerable amount and enticing to a seller. This letter can be more obvious in its sales effort to get the seller to agree to give you the mortgage.

■ *KEY POINT:*   *The letter to the owner can sell more.*

Other information in this book, particularly in Chapter 6, will give you numerous ideas of structuring mortgages with sellers.

This proposal is almost a requirement in buying a commercial or investment property. The seller of an income property is a businessperson who is more familiar with financial proposals and more experienced at constructing an arrangement giving you back a mortgage.

■ *KEY POINT:*   *A proposal detailing your financial information is needed by the seller of investment property.*

Often you can get a definite commitment from an individual seller on a mortgage request immediately. The written proposal outlining your formal request is designed to ensure the minimal amount of time necessary for a seller to make up his or her mind. As with a bank, it is your best chance for getting a favorable decision in the fastest possible amount of time.

■ *KEY POINT:*   *A proposal accompanying a purchase offer often guarantees a quick decision by the seller.*

LETTER TO SELLER

Mr. Jack Thompson

Dear Mr. Thompson,

Thank you for showing me your property last week. It's a fine house and shows the care you and Mrs. Thompson have given it over the years.

I would like to do what I can to purchase your home. You're asking $79,000, which is reasonable if I can be helped. Bank financing is very scarce with high interest rates this year. For me to purchase, I would like to ask you if I could take over your existing loan, which as you told me has a balance of $34,000 at an interest rate of 8½% with 12 years left to pay. Further, if you could lend me a second mortgage of $29,000, I could pay you 11% interest. I have myself and what I can get from other sources just under $16,000, a substantial amount of equity, to put down.

I know you didn't expect to give someone a second mortgage, but I hope to make it attractive to you. The interest rate of 11% is better than most money-market opportunities and guarantees you income each month. This second is backed by the security of your property. Also if you will agree to a payment period of 20 years so my monthly payments will not be too high, I will agree to pay this loan balance off in 6 years or sooner if I can refinance the balance of both loans at 10% or less.

I include a financial statement showing my income and expenses and assets and liabilities to show you I can meet payments on both loans.

I know you're anxious to move to your daughter's home in Minnesota. If my proposal is agreeable, you can start packing. I'll be ready to close within the week.

Sincerely,

Figure 1.5. Letter to seller.

How to Finance a Property in any Market

Writing a mortgage proposal is valuable in any economic climate. When mortgage money is plentiful, it will help you negotiate the best interest rate. When money is tight, it will help you get the best deal with the seller.

Either way, in good times or bad, your best assurance in securing a favorable decision on a mortgage request, whether it involves a bank or seller, is to outline specific written terms addressing major points to satisfy the lender. Security of the property, ability to repay the loan, and acknowledgment that it is profitable are the three points essential in negotiating a loan under any market conditions; often, in addressing them, they can help you get the best deal on a mortgage, while someone else does not.

■ *KEY POINT: A mortgage proposal helps negotiate a loan when funds are scarce.*

HOW YOU CAN ALWAYS GET YOUR MORTGAGE

The best way for you to ensure that you will get your mortgage is to be forthright and persistent. Forthright in that you are open with the financial information the seller or mortgage lender will need to act upon giving you a mortgage commitment. Absolute honesty is essential in your financial disclosure statement as well as appraisal information you present that backs up the value of the property. If a banker thinks that you have inflated figures or made other exaggerations he or she is likely to use extensive information at his or her disposal to discredit your presentation and in turn reject your request. It is almost better to understate things so that in the mind of the lender you have even more credibility than apparent.

■ *KEY POINT: Forthrightness and honesty gain credibility with the bank.*

The other way to ensure that you will get a mortgage is persistence. You must show the lender, whether an institution or seller, that you are anxious for his or her favorable approval. You don't need to overwhelm, but you should let them know that you are always available to provide more information, be interviewed by them, and help them should they wish to verify the information you have given.

■ *KEY POINT: Persistence keeps bankers conscious of your interest.*

At your initial meeting with the banker, when you first sit down with him or her, ask about what loans and terms such as interest rates might be available. At this time you may or may not have found the right property. Even before you find what you want, it's good to start shopping for the bank that offers the best terms and interest rates.

■ *KEY POINT: Preliminary shopping for a loan yields information and personal contacts.*

If you can establish what bank you wish to do business with before you buy, so much the better. Comparison shopping on types of loans and their terms and conditions will help you decide. Often you need to be persistent in getting the one with which you can make the best deal. Make contact, then, with as many loan officers in your area as you can. This book describes many different kinds of mortgages and their conditions to help you negotiate with a bank or seller.

THE SECRET OF GETTING A QUICK MORTGAGE

The way to best ensure you will get a mortgage commitment from a bank is to negotiate before you decide on the property. If you decide on the bank in which you would like to do business before you buy and conclude preliminary negotiations, such as type of loan and interest rates and other conditions, including discussion of your financial situation, when the time comes to ask for a particular mortgage you don't have to begin from scratch in negotiating with a lender. You've already done the majority of the work needed.

■ *KEY POINT:* *Shop for the loan before you contract to buy property.*

At this point you've laid the groundwork for getting a favorable decision. Once you choose the property, all you need to do is to assure the lender that the purchase price of the property is reasonable and that the loan doesn't conflict with the bank's lending guidelines.

This may sound simple, but it is the most effective way to ensure a quick mortgage commitment. It's done by the professional investors who wouldn't think of negotiating for a property without first having talked with a mortgage lender about what parameters within which mortgages are given and the interest rates and terms available.

■ *KEY POINT:* *Professionals always shop first.*

More and more individual, nonprofessional bank customers are taking this approach. Whether you are buying a single-family house, vacation home, or investment property for the first time, initially establishing a working relationship with a mortgage lender and then following up with a formal proposal when the right property is found is the best way to ensure obtaining a mortgage.

■ *KEY POINT:* *Establish contact with the banker before buying and submitting a formal proposal.*

When you go back to the lender, upon deciding upon a specific property, you are not a stranger. He or she knows something of your financial condition. You, in turn, know in a general way what terms are available—types of loans and interest rates—so a decision will be forthcoming much more quickly than if you walked into the bank and started from scratch. It is one of your best assurances that your loan request will be granted in the quickest amount of time.

Being prepared can also help you lock in an interest rate. Lenders have been known to delay completing paperwork because they know rates are about to be raised; by delaying they impose a higher rate. But by being prepared with an adequate proposal you give the lender no reason to delay, thus protecting yourself against the higher rate. You have done the lender's work for him by coming to the table fully prepared. Nothing could be a better negotiating point for locking in the lowest possible interest rate.

■ *KEY POINT:* *Preliminary contact with the banker helps ensure quick approval.*

In this chapter you have shared many secrets for how to get an immediate, favorable mortgage. They are principles borrowed from the pros. They are good practices to follow in shopping for a mortgage. Your persistence in finding the best bank with which to do business and beginning preliminary negotiations before you purchase—satisfying a lender and assuring him or her of the value of the property, your ability to repay the loan, its mutual profitability—go a long way toward ensuring a favorable and quick mortgage commitment.

In the next chapter we will talk about the chief types of mortgages and how each works so you can pick the best one.

ALL YOU NEED TO 2
KNOW ABOUT
MORTGAGES

To negotiate a speedy mortgage commitment you need some basic knowledge about which mortgages are available and which might work best for you. This chapter describes the major types of mortgages.

THE BASICS OF MORTGAGE FINANCING

A mortgage is a loan secured by property—a borrowing of money. The mortgage agreement, held by a bank or seller, is a promise to a lender—bank or seller—that you will repay the loan including the accrued interest. The property you purchase is the major part of the security for the repayment of this loan.

■ *KEY POINT: A mortgage is a loan on a property.*

■ *KEY POINT: A mortgage agreement is the promise to repay.*

The buyer of the property is the borrower, called the mortgagor, the one who gives the mortgage as pledge for repayment. The lender receiving this pledge is the mortgagee who holds the mortgage and receives payment on it from the one who is mortgaging or pledging the property.

■ *KEY POINT: The borrower gives the mortgage as pledge for repayment.*

The lender records the mortgage with the Registry of Deeds, or other governmental depository, as a legal document. This notice states that if the terms of the mortgage are not met, such as failing to repay on schedule or selling the property, the holder of the mortgage (the lender) is provided a legal way, usually called foreclosure, to take possession of the property to satisfy the indebtedness.

■ *KEY POINT: Mortgages are recorded in legal depositories.*

■ *CAUTION NOTE: Upon default, foreclosure is a legal way for lender to claim property.*

The loan lasts until the principal amount of the money plus interest is paid off. Then the mortgage is dissolved and the property is owned free and clear by the borrower.

■ *KEY POINT: The loan is dissolved when paid in full.*

THE BIG FOUR: THE FOUR BASIC TYPES OF MORTGAGES

How Conventional Mortgages Work

The majority of mortgages are called conventional mortgage loans. These include standard fixed rate and variable rate loans, both of which can be negotiated with a lending institution or the seller from whom you are buying the property.

The conventional mortgage doesn't carry any government guarantee. The loan is created by direct negotiation between you and a private bank or seller.

■ *KEY POINT:* *Conventional bank mortgages are private contracts.*

Most conventional mortgages have fixed interest rates that are constant throughout the term of the mortgage. The monthly payment doesn't vary for the life of the loan. The knowledge that payments will never rise, that is, not being dependent on general economic conditions, gives you a measure of security.

■ *KEY POINT:* *Fixed interest and equal payments add up to security.*

A conventional mortgage has a fixed rate of interest. This means that if your first monthly payment is $535, it will be the same 20 years from now. This offers financial consistency. Each year an amount of inflation eats away at the value of the dollar. It's easier in each succeeding year to get the money to make this fixed payment. A difficult amount in the first few years will be easier and easier to pay as time goes on.

■ *KEY POINT:* *Fixed payments offer financial consistency.*

The disadvantage is that the mortgage is based on fixed interest rates. If interest rates go up over the term of the mortgage you benefit, if they go down you lose.

■ *CAUTION NOTE:* *Fixed rates are bad for borrowers when rates go down.*

Sometimes you can renegotiate a conventional fixed mortgage should interest rates go lower than your present rate. But unless there is a substantial difference, special charges such as "points" may not make it worthwhile.

■ *KEY POINT:* *Conventional loans can be renegotiated.*

Another aspect to the conventional fixed rate mortgage is that the amount of interest paid during the early years of the mortgage greatly exceeds the amount of principal in each monthly payment. In fact, in the beginning this interest is almost the entire payment. In later years this shifts and the principal part of the payment far exceeds interest.

■ *CAUTION NOTE: In the beginning years of a loan, interest greatly exceeds principal.*

The accompanying chart shows how a conventional mortgage works over a term of 25 years. You can use this chart as a guide in comparing it with other forms of mortgages. You'll notice you need to reach some years into the mortgage before you begin to start to pay off much of the balance. Although it took the full 25 years to pay off the original amount you borrowed, a substantial amount of interest was paid over the full term. This will

---

CONVENTIONAL MORTGAGE

Payment of principal and interest in a fixed rate, conventional loan: $65,000 mortgage for 25 years at 10% interest.

Year	Annual Payment	Interest	Principal	Balance
1	$7,160.92	$6,500.00	$660.92	$64,339
2	$7,160.92	$6,433.91	$727.01	$63,612
3	$7,160.92	$6,361.21	$799.71	$62,812
4	$7,160.92	$6,281.24	$879.68	$61,932
5	$7,160.92	$6,193.27	$967.65	$60,965
10	$7,160.92	$5,602.51	$1,558.41	$54,990
15	$7,160.92	$4,651.08	$2,509.84	$44,720
20	$7,160.92	$3,118.79	$4,042.13	$27,820
25	$7,160.92	$651.03	$6,510.35	0

Note: Principal does not become more than interest in the monthly payment until just before the 20th year.

Figure 2.1. Chart on conventional mortgage.

be a useful tool when used in comparison with other mortgage plans.

How ARMs Work

The high interest rates of the late 1970s and early 1980s spurred the creation of different kinds of mortgages. Not only was money to lend out relatively scarce but demand went down in proportion to the higher rate. To soften the blow of the higher rates banks invented some ingenious devices, and in so doing, sought to protect themselves.

One of the more popular, at least among the bankers, was known as the adjustable rate mortgage, or ARM. Many new borrowers found themselves confronted with this new mortgage. They had little choice, banks made it easy to borrow this way and penalized those who still wanted a fixed rate.

■ *CAUTION NOTE: Banks invented adjustable mortgages to protect themselves.*

How does it work? It's similar to the conventional mortgage except the rate of interest varies according to economic conditions. For example, if the interest rate you negotiate at the beginning of your mortgage is 16% and economic conditions, such as the supply of money, increased manufacturing ability, more trade with other countries, or simply lower taxes, cause the average cost of borrowing money to go down, the rate charged on a mortgage might drop to 14%.

The indicator chosen to monitor interest rates could be various governmental indices, depending upon which one is chosen by your bank. For example, the 90-day Treasury Bill, the interest rate the U.S. Treasury paid on short-term bonds, is a common index.

■ *KEY POINT: Adjustable rate mortgages vary accordingly to national indicators.*

It's hard to look at the adjustable rate mortgage objectively and see it for what it is. We're barraged with much favorable advertising sponsored by the banks. In addition, this type of mortgage did not enjoy a period of time during which it could be tested. After all, when it started rates were high, and in the last few years rates have dropped off. What will happen when rates rise? There may be a lot of disappointed borrowers who will be hurt if they must start paying more each month.

The banks like ARMs in times when interest rates are high. It promotes the loaning of money. Loans that couldn't be made because the interest rate was too high can often be negotiated if borrowers convince themselves rates will drop. And, as economic conditions improve, they tend to do so. The average interest rates of 16–18% have dropped into the range of 12–14%. What borrowers tend to forget is that the opposite can happen too. When the general interest goes up, it can affect a mortgage by causing a dramatic jump in payments.

■ *CAUTION NOTE: Banks benefit with ARMs by passing on a rising interest rate.*

■ *KEY POINT: Borrowers benefit when rates fall.*

But these are only words of caution. Like any mortgage, you get what you pay for. There are some decided advantages in opting for the ARM.

The exact terms and conditions of an ARM must be looked into before any final decision can be made on whether it is best for you. Much can vary in an ARM, not only as to what national indicator the interest rate is tied to, but also as to the percentage that the mortgage can jump at any one time. For example, the indicators may jump 2% during a six-month period, but the conditions of your mortgage only allow the bank to increase your interest rate 1%. This takes some of the sting out of the overall rise.

■ *CAUTION NOTE:* *Always study specific conditions that make rates rise or fall.*

Be aware that, just as oil prices affect gasoline costs at the pump, banks are fairly efficient at promptly notifying you of increases in the interest rate but tend to be slower in negotiating your payment downward.

■ *CAUTION NOTE:* *Banks are quick to raise the rate but slow to lower it.*

You must be constantly vigilant. Sometimes, the slightly lower cost, for example, by a percentage point or two, of an adjustable rate mortgage is not always better than a conventional fixed rate. If you only benefit by two points lower than the fixed rate you should be cautioned that what seems like an advantage must be compared with security of a fixed payment that will not vary regardless of the economic times. True, payments of the ARM may be more moderate in the beginning, but may not remain easy to pay as time goes on. At least in theory, adjustable rate payments of loans negotiated today could in future years skyrocket.

■ *KEY POINT:* *The initially lower interest in an ARM must be weighed against the long-term stability of fixed rate loan.*
■ *CAUTION NOTE:* *Protection is needed against ARM rates skyrocketing.*

However, in knowing their problems, you are armed in negotiating an ARM to work for your advantage. If an initially lower interest rate is important to you, and it should be, you can guard against harsh changes.

Protection for substantial upward swing in the interest rate and payments is provided for in some ARM agreements. Some of these terms are either automatically within the mortgage agreement or can be negotiated into it by you. For example, the maximum amount that interest or payments can be increased each year should always be stated in an ARM agreement.

■ *KEY POINT: Negotiate the maximum upward swing.*

A chart is included here to help you gauge the cost of an ARM.

Comparing how an ARM works with a conventional mortgage, you might initially decide that if interest rates go up, you'd prefer to get a fixed rate loan and lock in the lower rate; however, if you think interest rates will go down, an adjustable

ARM MORTGAGE

Beginning interest of 10% on an adjustable rate mortgage of $65,000 for 25 years

Year	Rate	Payment	Interest	Principal	Balance
1	10.0%	$7,160	$6,500	$660	$64,339
2	10.5%	$7,364	$6,856	$509	$63,830
3	10.5%	$7,364	$6,649	$715	$63,115
4	11.0%	$7,645	$7,060	$585	$62,530
5	11.5%	$7,929	$7,344	$585	$61,945
10	12.0%	$8,215	$6,980	$1,235	$57,070
15	11.5%	$7,929	$5,589	$2,340	$46,995
20	13.0%	$8,797	$4,507	$4,290	$32,240
25	12.5%	$8,505	$575	$7,930	0

Figure 2.2. Chart on adjustable rate mortgage.

rate mortgage would be preferable. There is some truth to this, but beware of looking at it this simply. Even the experts who suggest the direction interest rates will take are often wrong. It is difficult to predict the future.

■ *CAUTION NOTE:*   *It is almost impossible to predict whether rates will rise or fall.*

Even the old adage that interest rates tend to rise when inflation is high and tend to fall when inflation eases is not always true. There are too many other factors that come into play, including world economic conditions, or corporate failure, all of which may affect interest rates.

This is not to take away from some of the obvious advantages of an ARM but to give a cautionary word that its popularity may lessen as interest rates become less stable for the long term and borrowers decide on the security of a fixed payment.

■ *CAUTION NOTE:*   *ARMs may become less popular as interest rates stabilize.*

In negotiating any loan with a variable payment, make sure that upward swings are limited, not only in amount but in the length of time in which they can be enacted. And make sure there is ultimately a cap on the upward increase in mortgage interests. For example, you might have a $600-a-month payment at the beginning of the loan and if you had to in two years you could handle an $800-a-month payment. But you may not want to be saddled with a $1200 monthly payment if your original 11% rate skyrockets to 19%.

■ *KEY POINT:*   *Negotiate a cap on how high interest rate can rise.*

So approach ARMs with care. It may be cheaper to renegotiate a conventional fixed rate of interest downward than to struggle with the uncertainty of a rising mortgage rate. With a fixed rate loan you can ensure stability, but you'd have to start with the $800 payment.

Advertised by banks as a great boon to consumers, ARMs more often benefit the lenders. You will learn more specifics about different types of adjustable rate loans in Chapter 5.

How Government Loans and Guarantees Work

The loans discussed in this book involve getting a mortgage from a bank or seller. However, when the government becomes involved in the loan process, a quick commitment is not always possible. It takes time for the government to move. One can speed the process up, but bringing in the government often means one to three weeks before approval can be gained.

■ *CAUTION NOTE: Commitment is slow in government-approved loans.*

The Federal Housing Administration (FHA) and the Veterans Administration (VA) have loan programs that require only a minimum cash down payment or in some cases none at all. The VA (more popularly known as "GI") loan is available for the purchase of homes. The VA loan protects the borrower in a number of ways. One way is in the amount of interest rate charged and the amount of money that you can borrow. These GI loans do not usually require any down payment unless the price of the house exceeds a particular limit. The FHA loan limit is often somewhat less than the GI loan. They require that a minimum of 3–5% down payment be made.

■ *KEY POINT: Only minimal down payments are required in government mortgages.*

A measure of security is afforded in a government loan. The interest rate set by the government is generally lower than the prevailing rates of the marketplace, and a government-approved loan appraiser must pass his or her often conservative judgment on your purchase.

■ *KEY POINT:* *The government has a rigid appraisal process.*

These loans can be difficult to negotiate. Banks simply don't like to make them because they can usually lend their money at a higher rate in a conventional mortgage. In practice, they have a guarantee from the government to be reimbursed should the borrower default, but as we mentioned earlier in the book, rarely do foreclosures take place unless the situation of the borrower is very dire.

■ *CAUTION NOTE:* *Banks shy away from government loans.*

When an institutional lender does make a loan of this type, they usually charge "points"—an extra two or three percentage points of the loan amount as a fee for making the loan. This increases the bank's yield and is only charged once to you. These factors must be taken into account when choosing the actual loan you may be eligible for.

■ *CAUTION NOTE:* *Extra percentage points based on the loan amount increase the bank's profit.*

How Seller Financing Works

One of the quickest ways to negotiate a mortgage commitment is to do business with the seller. Professional investors often do this with owners of commercial and residential buildings. In this era of high interest rates it has also become popular with consumers buying smaller properties.

■ *KEY POINT:* *High rates have made seller financing popular.*

Often a bank is approached on an as-need-to basis just in case negotiations on financing with the seller should fail.

It's becoming more and more common for a seller of a home to participate in financing. In many cases, particularly if the seller has no current mortgage indebtedness on the property and owns it free and clear, you are in an excellent position to gain the seller's help.

■ *KEY POINT:*   *"Free-and-clear" property facilitates seller financing.*

The seller could give you the entire first mortgage. For example, a retired couple moving to a vacation area might like to hold a mortgage at current interest rates. Not only may they benefit tax-wise—not having to pay, through an installment sale (see Chapter 8), their income tax on the sale until the year in which they receive payment—but the money they will receive over the term of the mortgage is secured by the value of their former house which they knew so well and loved.

■ *KEY POINT:*   *When giving a mortgage, the seller's taxes can be spread out.*

Usually the seller makes the decision to help you financially at the same time the terms of the sale itself are negotiated. You simply include in your purchase offer the condition that the seller take back all or a portion of the mortgage. The short-form purchase agreement commonly used in the United States illustrates the way in which you make this offer.

■ *KEY POINT:*   *The deal on seller financing is negotiated at the same time as the sale.*

This seller becomes the lender. Loans with the seller are usually conventional with fixed rates of interest. Rarely will the seller be sophisticated enough to deal with the complexities of

OFFER-TO-PURCHASE AGREEMENT

Date _____

I, _____, offer $_____ as a deposit on your property at _____ for the purchase price of $_____ to be returned to me if not accepted before _____. If accepted, in addition to this deposit I will put down the balance of ___% within 10 days and will close on or before _____. Additional terms and conditions: Sale conditional upon buyer receiving financial approval from a local mortgage bank on or before _____. Seller will give buyer second mortgage for 8% of purchase price at 12% interest for 5 years.

Buyer	Seller

Figure 2.3. Short-form purchase agreement. (*Note:* Financing can be made part of a purchase offer).

giving you a swinging interest rate and variable payments. But an adjustable loan may not be best for you if you decide to finance with the seller.

■ *CAUTION NOTE:* *Seller financing is usually at a conventional fixed rate.*

The seller is not a professional lender. You may have versed yourself in the various types of mortgages and beneficial conditions for financial institutions, but for the seller it's a one-time deal. To avoid confusion in the seller's mind you must carefully spell out the terms and benefits the seller will gain. More on seller financing in Chapter 6.

■ *KEY POINT:* *Keep the financing proposal to the seller simple.*

When the seller takes the whole mortgage, you don't have to conjure up detailed information, such as comparable sales, on the value of the property. You may disclose to the seller some assumptions of financial conditions, but you avoid the paperwork required and often the more formal negotiations involved with an institutional lender. Getting the seller to take back the mortgage is the easiest and quickest way to secure a mortgage commitment.

■ *KEY POINT: You only detail your financial situation to the seller.*

Specific ways of financing that can be arranged to benefit you and the seller are described in more detail in Chapter 6 on getting the seller to give you the mortgage.

INNOVATIVE TECHNIQUES OF CREATIVE FINANCING

They say necessity is the mother of invention; it is no less true about financing. There are so many different ways to arrange the financing of real estate—houses, a second home, investment property, or land—that one would have to write an encyclopedia to tell about them all.

Many innovative techniques on creative financing are discussed in this book. They all have different names and angles that make them unique. The key in benefiting you is to see which one will save you money. For example, one of the more common techniques is to combine conventional bank financing with additional help from the seller. You may negotiate a fixed rate or adjustable rate mortgage with a bank for 8% of the purchase price and negotiate with the seller for another 10–15% as a second mortgage. This is desirable for the seller and it allows him or her to facilitate the sale of the property and gain some extra money in the form of interest over the term of the second mortgage. Second mortgages are usually far shorter term than an institutional loan and perhaps a point more in interest than the average current mortgage interest rate.

■ *KEY POINT: Creative financing usually involves a combination of seller and bank financing.*

You, however, benefit in that it reduces your cash requirement for purchasing the house down to 5–10% of the selling price. In this way you conserve your cash for needed improvements or as a reserve to help make future mortgage payments.

■ *KEY POINT: You can often commit less cash as a down payment through creative financing.*

The second mortgage by the seller is the simplest form of creating financing. It is also the most common and easy to negotiate. Other techniques you've probably heard of, such as assuming the mortgage, purchase money mortgages, blanket mortgages, wraparounds, even the option with contract to buy, are only some of the innovative techniques that will be discussed in this book—all of which can be negotiated in a short amount of time.

■ *KEY POINT: Second mortgages are a common way to finance creatively.*

What you need to do is choose from several alternatives and then tailor one or two of these to best fit you and the seller. For example, you buy a ten-unit apartment building for $300,000 on which there already is a $180,000 first mortgage, a loan you cannot take over under the laws of your state. However, you are able to negotiate a wraparound mortgage with a minimal down payment of $10,000. The seller, in turn, gives you a mortgage of $290,000 on which you will be making monthly payments to him. He, in turn, sends the portion of your monthly payment on the existing non-assumable loan of $180,000 to the bank which holds it.

■ *KEY POINT:* *A wraparound mortgage can often work when you can't assume an existing loan.*

This is similar to your taking over the responsibility of the existing mortgage and the seller giving you a second mortgage of $110,000. But often it is not technically possible to assume these first loans; this is why we present another way to do the same thing.

■ *CAUTION NOTE:* *Many existing mortgages are not assumable.*

The wraparound makes the deal. From the seller's point of view the wraparound mortgage is secured by the property, and just like the bank the seller is only interested in the portion of the mortgage he holds.

Creative and rapid financing of mortgages comes from awareness of the various ways to arrange them.

MORTGAGING A HOME VERSUS AN INVESTMENT PROPERTY

Before we detail the many sources of mortgage money and various ways you can make financing work, let's understand what we're using this money for. Specifically, do these techniques work for buying a home, investment property, or a piece of land? One of the great myths about buying real estate is that you finance each property with different types of loans. Nothing could be further from the truth.

■ *KEY POINT:* *Mortgage loans are basically the same for all types of properties.*

The tight money and high interest rates of just a few years ago brought forth some intricate financial devices. They were used not only by purchasers of income and commercial property but also home buyers. Financing an investment property is rarely different from financing a house. In many investment properties, even multi-unit apartment projects, financing is of the conventional type, although several banks may be participating as one to pool the large funds needed.

■ *KEY POINT:* *On large properties several banks may combine their funds into one mortgage.*

Even in the purchase of a house, the seller, more often than not, is willing to give financial help to a responsible buyer.

■ *KEY POINT:* *Sellers are often willing to give financing.*

This book is not only about the many intricacies of conventional or creative financing; its main thrust concerns the negotiations between buyer and lender that must take place to get a mortgage commitment. If you are aware of which financial technique will benefit you and can present it in a simple manner to the lender or seller, you have your best chance of gaining favorable approval.

■ *KEY POINT:* *Financing is negotiating a particular technique.*

HOW TO DECIDE WHETHER SHORT OR LONG TERM WORKS BEST FOR YOU

All mortgages, whether from a bank or seller, whether conventional or creative, have a length of time over which payments are made to satisfy the debt. Once a standard mortgage was 20 to 25 years. In recent years mortgages have crept up to 30 years or more. Many people have opted for these longer-term mortgages as they spread the loan out a longer time, making the payments slightly less.

■ *KEY POINT:* *Longer-term payment schedules mean lower payments.*

However, be aware that at some point you will want the principal balance on the loan paid. As you saw in Chapter 1, the amount of the monthly payment reducing the overall loan balance, or principal, does not become a significant portion of the monthly payment until the later stages of the mortgage. Many investors look at income property on the basis that it generates enough cash to meet the requirements of shorter payoff. They plan on holding their property for a while and don't want to pay off the tremendous amount of interest due over a 30-year term. They seek to pay off a 15- or even 12-year loan.

■ *CAUTION NOTE:* *More interest is paid in a long-term loan.*

■ *KEY POINT:* *Principal is paid off more quickly in a short-term loan.*

The same is true with a house. If you can afford the higher payments of a shorter 15- or 20-year mortgage, you will get to the point where you bring down your indebtedness much more rapidly than in a longer loan.

Your monthly payment is higher, but as the following chart shows, the differences between the payments in a 30-year and 20-year loan are not as great as you might think. And look at how much less interest you pay over the whole term. The interest paid over the period of the loan is much less when the mortgage is for a shorter term.

There can be a dramatic difference in the reduction of principal balance in a shorter-term mortgage. Note that not until the 24th year in the 30-year loan have you paid off more than 50% of the

THE LONG-TERM VERSUS THE SHORT-TERM MORTGAGE

$75,000 mortgage for 30 years at 11½% compared with the same loan amount and percentage for 15 years.

Monthly payments: 15-year loan = $867.18
30-year loan = $742.73

Remaining balance in percent of original loan amount

Age of Loan	Original Term	
	15 Years	30 Years
1	97.3	99.6
2	94.4	99.1
3	91.0	98.6
4	87.3	98.1
5	83.1	97.4
7	73.1	95.9
9	60.5	94.0
11	44.8	91.6
13	24.9	88.6
15	0.0	84.8

Figure 2.4. Chart on long-term versus short-term mortgage.

original loan—more than 9 years after you paid the loan off under the 15-year plan!

This does not mean that longer term mortgages are bad for you. Most property, whether a home or investment, is not held for the duration of the loan. The average family moves every four to five years, their requirements constantly changing. Investment properties are usually held for longer periods.

■ *KEY POINT: The average holding period for residential property is less than five years.*

Your situation is unique. The money you have available for payments must set the guidelines as to whether you opt for a shorter- or longer-term mortgage.

■ *KEY POINT:* *The money for payments often decides the length of term of the mortgage.*

WHAT TERMS YOU SHOULD ALWAYS HAVE IN A MORTGAGE AGREEMENT

In buying a property, whether a home or for investment, price and terms are intricately interwoven. For example, if you pay $100,000 for a property and the seller carries back a mortgage of $90,000 at two points below the going interest rate, you've gotten a bargain. In this case the current interest rate is 15%, but you only pay 13% on the $90,000. This difference of 2% based on the $90,000 means that you are paying much less in overall cost for the property.

Any time you can negotiate a lower interest rate than prevailing rate, it's like paying that much less for the property.

■ *KEY POINT:* *Less interest means less overall cost.*

A major consideration in keeping your mortgage costs down is "points." These points are based on the amount of the mortgage. For example, three points are three percentage points of your mortgage. If you obtain a $40,000 mortgage, you will pay $4,000 just as a fee to originate the loan.

■ *CAUTION NOTE:* *Percentage "points" are extra fees charged to you upon originating a loan.*

Each bank may decide whether or not they charge points. They may do so upon either the initiation of the mortgage or upon any prepayment. Several years from now when you may need to sell, you don't want the bank to charge you an extra 2–3% — points based on the balance of the mortgage — as a fee for paying off the loan.

■ *CAUTION NOTE: Prepayment points may be charged on the balance at the time you pay off the loan.*

If a lender with whom you wish to do business does charge points on prepayment, insist there be some limit in time after which the points will no longer be charged. For example, if the loan is held for four years, the four-point penalty will drop down to two, and then at six years no prepayment penalty will be charged.

■ *KEY POINT: Insist on time limits when prepayment points are no longer charged.*

One thing making points particularly odious is that they are often charged for fixed rate loans and not for ARMs. Doesn't that tell you that banks want to lend their money on variable payment plans? More on negotiating points downward in the following chapters.

■ *CAUTION NOTE: Points are more commonly charged with conventional fixed rate loans.*

Lenders often wish to add personal insurance—life and disability insurance tied to the mortgage balance. This type of insurance is often expensive, particularly if it is the "whole life" not the "term" variety. However, as a borrower about to make a large financial commitment you should ensure that your family is protected with enough life and disability insurance. As an alternative to mortgage-tied policies (which are expensive gimmicks), you are better off reviewing your current coverage and updating policies.

Any time you can allow someone else to assume your mortgage in the future you will get a distinct advantage. Several years from now you may want to pass this assumable mortgage on to someone else.

■ *KEY POINT: It's a great advantage if in the future your mortgage can be assumed by someone else.*

Making a new loan assumable is more difficult to negotiate than points, but not always impossible. Banks have lobbied for laws to stop loans from being assumed. In some states banks are willing to allow a second party to assume payment on a loan, particularly if they have the right to judge the credit-worthiness of the new borrower. However, the name of the first borrower often remains on the loan in addition to the name of the new borrower.

■ *KEY POINT: Many loans can be assumed legally.*

Other terms and conditions vary with the type of mortgage. A conventional mortgage with a fixed rate of interest and period of time is straightforward in comparison with an adjustable plan. If you have an ARM or some variation (discussed in Chapter 5), such as changing payments, make sure there are no terms in your mortgage agreement that penalize you beyond the normal principal and interest you are obligated to pay.

■ *KEY POINT: Limit charges to interest and principal only.*

Terms can vary as much as the many kinds and ways to arrange a mortgage. A blanket mortgage, for example, which we will talk about in the next chapter, is when you put up additional property as security for a new loan. If it makes sense for you to arrange your loan this way, negotiate a time limit. For example, you don't want two properties pledged together for the full term of a mortgage. At some point, perhaps in as soon as three years, the value of the property you are buying will increase enough so that the property pledge as security can be dropped from the blanket loan agreement.

■ *CAUTION NOTE: Negotiate time limits to release secured property from blanket loans.*

These are only some of the many terms you must negotiate to protect yourself. And you can't rely on anyone besides yourself to negotiate the best deal for you. You can't expect the bank to look out for you. The real estate agent just wants the deal and rarely can do more than steer you to different banks. Your lawyer can help but even he or she is more oriented to preparing the deed and searching the title than arranging your mortgage. It's expected you will negotiate the mortgage. Nobody is likely to give you more than advice. You've got to talk to the bank.

■ *CAUTION NOTE: You are the best person to negotiate terms.*

Banks, however, are not difficult to do business with. Most banks have guidelines that are not unreasonable. Some are more flexible than others. A bank often differs from other banks on the terms they're willing to negotiate. And banks in one area may have similar but different policies from those in other areas.

■ *KEY POINT: Banks are easy to work with.*

It may seem like all bankers get together on what they'll charge for interest. They really don't. It's illegal for them to set policy among themselves in regard to what they charge or what they pay out to their depositors. Good news for consumers, but the similarity in what they charge is more due to their having to borrow from larger banks, which in turn borrow from even more central banks.

■ *KEY POINT: Banks cannot get together and set rates.*

More flexibility in banking practices come in the terms and conditions under which money is lent out. Here is where you have the room to negotiate the most advantageous mortgage.

WHEN TO TURN TO PROFESSIONALS

When it's advice you need, you can get some help from professionals. Even if you are buying a property on which the seller is going to give you back the mortgage, it doesn't hurt to sit down with your local neighborhood banker and get some idea of what loans and terms might be available from his or her institution. This may help you in negotiating with the seller.

■ *KEY POINT: Preliminary contact with bankers helps in negotiating later.*

Bankers want to loan you money. That's their job—to act as a salesperson for their bank. They have to get loans out the door. Many times they're very willing to help in negotiating around the complex conditions offered by that bank. The disadvantage is that they may be prejudiced to the bank's position. True, their advice is often less than objective, but talking to several bankers will give you an overall picture of the terms and conditions you can negotiate.

■ *KEY POINT: Valuable information comes from personal contact.*

Other professionals include local real estate agents. You may be using one in your purchase. His or her advice can be invaluable in negotiating a loan, particularly with a seller.

Again, if you must take the real estate agent's advice, do so with caution, particularly if he or she is involved in selling you the property in question. You may end up with mortgage terms that are not really desirable. However, since they negotiate mortgages all the time for many different buyers, their advice on what types of loans and terms and conditions are available can prove invaluable—all information gained before you even visit the bank.

■ *KEY POINT: Real estate salespeople are savvy negotiators of mortgage terms and conditions.*

Your lawyer—always have a lawyer—in buying any property can help, particularly if you and the bank are stuck. Also, the negotiation of a loan from a seller needs to be written up into a formal document.

■ *KEY POINT: Your lawyer can help negotiate a difficult problem.*

A new category of professional counselor is called a real estate counselor or advisor. These are people with experience in real estate who for a fee act as an objective advisor. They don't sell property but help you with a specific problem such as having a property surveyed or when to sell. They can also help you get a mortgage.

Instead of acting like an agent pledging to a seller, they work for you. They act on your behalf.

Since they are not getting a commission on the sale of the property, they work for a flat fee, which varies according to the kind of advice and the amount of time needed to help you. Fees can range anywhere from $50 to $150 for advice on negotiating a mortgage.

■ *KEY POINT: Real estate counselors work on your behalf in negotiating different types of mortgages.*

If you need someone locally, the real estate counselor may be the best person. Compared with the others, his or her advice should be the most objective.

In the next chapter we will examine the different sources from which you can get your mortgage.

3

DECIDING HOW MUCH YOU CAN AFFORD

Deciding how much you as a borrower can afford is one of the first steps in getting a mortgage. This chapter offers some guidelines to help you decide on a comfortable range of affordability.

HOW MUCH CAN YOU AFFORD?

How big a mortgage you can afford has a lot to do with how much you can spend on a house. The following table is a guide to help you decide how much house you'll be able to afford, given your income and a variety of interest rates. The table assumes you will make a 10% cash down payment and that monthly payments for mortgage, property taxes, and insurance will equal 30% of your gross income.

You will notice in Figure 3.1 how much less you can afford for each rise in interest rate. For example, in the $70,000 income row, the difference between paying a mortgage of 9% and paying one of 13% is $50,000 in the amount of house you can afford.

■ *CAUTION NOTE: Each rise in interest rate dramatically increases cost.*

A guideline of how much you can afford. Income brackets and possible interest rates are given. The table assumes you make a 10% down payment and that monthly payments for your mortgage will equal 30% of your gross income. Property taxes and insurance equal 5%.

Taxes/ Ins.	Income Range	Monthly Payment Available	House cost at 25-year fixed rate				
			9%	10%	11%	12%	13%
$1,500	$ 30,000	$ 625.00	$ 74,494	68,758	63,776	59,354	55,408
2,000	40,000	833.33	99,325	91,676	85,034	79,139	73,877
2,500	50,000	1,041.67	124,156	114,595	106,293	98,924	92,346
3,000	60,000	1,250.00	148,987	137,514	127,551	118,708	110,816
3,500	70,000	1,458.33	173,818	160,433	148,810	138,493	129,285
4,000	80,000	1,666.67	198,649	183,352	170,068	158,278	147,754
4,500	90,000	1,875.00	223,480	206,271	191,327	178,063	166,223
5,000	100,000	2,083.33	248,331	229,190	212,585	197,847	184,693

Figure 3.1. How much can you afford?

SHOP FOR THE BEST RATES

Surprisingly, mortgage rates can vary widely, and as you can see by the affordability chart in Figure 3.1, interest rates can be critical in making it financially possible for you to pay a mortgage. For example, payments on a 10½% $90,000, 25-year fixed rate loan are $849.60 a month, compared with $914 for the same loan at 11½%.

An 8½% ARM would mean initial payments of $725 a month, but inevitably these ARM payments will rise in the future. As you can see by the Payment Table in Figure 3.2 that shows monthly payments for each $1,000 borrowed, payments climb at each higher interest rate.

Look down the interest rate column in the payment table in Figure 3.2 for the rate at which you wish to calculate the monthly payment, and across to the right for the mortgage term columns, 15 through 30 years. The amount shown is the monthly payment

Monthly Payments per $1,000 borrowed

Interest rate	15 years	20 years	25 years	30 years
8.00	$ 9.56	$ 8.36	$ 7.79	$ 7.34
8.25	9.70	8.52	7.89	7.51
8.50	9.85	8.68	8.06	7.69
8.75	9.99	8.84	8.22	7.87
9.00	10.14	9.00	8.39	8.05
9.25	10.29	9.16	8.56	8.23
9.50	10.44	9.32	8.74	8.41
9.75	10.59	9.49	8.91	8.59
10.00	10.75	9.65	9.09	8.78
10.25	10.90	9.82	9.26	8.97
10.50	11.06	9.98	9.44	9.15
10.75	11.21	10.15	9.62	9.34
11.00	11.37	10.32	9.80	9.53
11.25	11.53	10.49	9.98	9.72
11.50	11.69	10.66	10.16	9.91
11.75	11.85	10.84	10.35	10.10
12.00	12.01	11.01	10.53	10.29
12.25	12.17	11.19	10.72	10.48
12.50	12.33	11.36	10.90	10.68
12.75	12.49	11.54	11.09	10.87
13.00	12.65	11.72	11.28	11.06
13.25	12.82	11.89	11.47	11.26
13.50	12.98	12.07	11.66	11.45
13.75	13.15	12.25	11.85	11.65

Figure 3.2. Payment table.

for each $1,000 borrowed. To find the monthly payment for a particular loan, simply divide that amount by 1,000 and multiply the result by the payment per $1,000. For example, if you need to borrow $85,000 for 25 years at 11.75%, go across the 11.75% row to the 25-year column; the payment shown is $10.35 per

$1,000. Your monthly payment, then, would be $879.75, or $10.35 times 85.

PRIVATE AND PUBLIC LOAN GUIDELINES

It is imperative that you understand how lenders will evaluate your loan application. Knowing what they are looking for allows you to match your needs to theirs. The chart Figure 3.2 uses 30% for interest and principal, property taxes, and insurance. This is an average figure that measures your borrowing power as a ratio of housing expenses to your gross household income.

■ *KEY POINT: Many lenders use 30% as a basic expense guideline.*

The federal government program FANNIE MAE uses such figures as 28 and 36%; specifically, the monthly mortgage interest and principal payments, plus property taxes and homeowner's insurance, should total no more than 28% of your gross monthly income. Additionally, your monthly house payments plus other long-term debts, such as automobile or student loans, should total no more than 36% of your gross income.

■ *CAUTION NOTE: Fannie Mae uses 28% as a limit for property expenses.*

Many banks follow these FANNIE MAE guidelines, as they often wish to repackage a group of loans and resell them. Income defined by FANNIE MAE is the work you have been doing for a year or longer, not the extra income you are getting from a part-time job you started last month. Even such extra income as bonuses, commissions, and overtime must be averaged for at least two years to be considered wages. Child support payments and alimony are only considered as income if the payments continue at least three years into the future.

■ *CAUTION NOTE:* *Lenders often wish to sell loans that meet Fannie Mae guidelines.*

To qualify for adjustable rate mortgages, the kind where you might face steep rate hikes in the future, you must meet even stricter requirements. If your ARM starts with a lower initial rate, such as 8% with a 2-percentage point maximum increase per year, capping out at 6% (over the term of the mortgage), FANNIE MAE, and in turn your lender, analyzes this mortgage based on a 10% rate.

In fact, if you wish to make a down payment of less than 10% of the purchase price, FANNIE MAE and your bank are likely to look at a stricter ratio of housing expense to income, such as 25 and 30%. That means that for a $91,000 loan on a $100,000 house, your payments cannot be more than one-quarter of your gross monthly income and your long term debt, no more than 33%.

These are not strict guidelines. Even FANNIE MAE treats every mortgage on its own merits. Many factors can tip the scales one way or another, and the most important factors in gaining a mortgage can be a good credit history, substantial down payment, and assets equal to at least three months of mortgage payments in reserve. Thus their 28% guideline often can reach 30% or more.

■ *CAUTION NOTE:* *Fannie Mae guidelines are usually more strict than individual bank policy.*

A rough guideline for you to follow is that monthly loan payments, including insurance and taxes, should equal 30% or less of your gross household income. Although many banks, such as those that sell their mortgages through the FANNIE MAE system, have a guideline of 28% or less, the rise in interest rates and overall housing costs have caused many lenders, as well as borrowers, to realize that they must allocate more for monthly housing costs than was once considered acceptable.

MAKING THE MOST OF YOUR BORROWING POWER

Start by analyzing your monthly expenses. As a general rule, if many of your long-term, basic expenses exceed 35% of your income, consider selling some assets, such as stocks or mutual fund shares, to pay off some of this debt. As with the down payment, seek help from family, relatives, or friends in cleaning up some of these debts.

■ *KEY POINT: Keep long-term debts to a reasonable limit.*

Often, as with the terms of a larger down payment and bringing some of your expenses up to date, the lender will demand written proof that any money you receive is a gift, not a disguised loan. Remember, the key thing with a lender is that you, without help from outside sources, are able to meet the new financial needs of owning a property.

■ *CAUTION NOTE: Sometimes, particularly if putting down a minimal down payment, the lender requires unborrowed money.*

ADJUSTING YOUR DOWN PAYMENT

Varying your down payment to meet your needs is one way to keep your monthly payments in line with what you can afford. If you have the cash or equity in an existing home, you can keep your mortgage loan at a minimum by making as high a down payment as possible on your new property.

At 10½% for 25 years, the difference between a $90,000 loan and a $75,000 loan is $142 per month. This is very helpful if you are buying for the second or third time and have equity built up in a previous property.

■ *KEY POINT: More down payment means less monthly cost.*

THE PROBLEM OF A LOW
DOWN PAYMENT

Often the biggest obstacle facing first-time homebuyers today is not getting a mortgage but getting a down payment together. Occasionally you can put down as little as 5% of the purchase price, but closer to 20% is common.

You should make sure that your down payment won't unduly restrict your other financial needs but will be large enough to keep down the amount of mortgage money needed. As you can see in the Affordability Chart in Figure 3.1, monthly mortgage payments can slip over $1,000 a month in a loan approaching $100,000 at 12%. Therefore, the more you are able to put down, the less you must borrow and the lower your monthly payments will be.

■ *CAUTION NOTE: A low down payment causes high monthly mortgage payments and restricts other needy purchases.*

It is true that many government-backed FHA loans for low- and middle-income homebuyers, and VA loans for veterans, allow homebuyers to make no down payment or a very low one. But putting as much down as possible means you not only secure your chances for getting a loan, but you minimize the amount of mortgage money you will need to borrow.

However, for those who don't have the equity of one house to put into the purchase of a new one, making the mortgage payments is easier compared to coming up with a big lump sum of cash for the down payment, points, and other closing costs.

MORTGAGE INSURANCE

A stipulation regularly required by the lender for borrowers putting down less than 20% is that they buy private mortgage insurance, usually available through the lender. This guarantees the loan until the equity in your home equals 20% of the fair market value. Federal mortgage insurance is included in FHA and VA loans.

■ *KEY POINT: Mortgage insurance is usually required for minimal down payments.*

In fact, this mortgage insurance, which varies between ½ and 1½% at the closing and adds $20 to $35 to the monthly payment on average, becomes more expensive the smaller your down payment gets.

Some lending institutions want to charge more points if you make a minimal down payment, so it is best to beg or borrow from your friends and family in order to put down at least 15% if not 20%. By doing so you minimize the number of points needed and eliminate private mortgage insurance, which makes quick approval of your mortgage application easier. Banks always have to look more closely at deals where the purchasing of property is made with less than 20% down, and they may take extra time to scrutinize credit and property value, delaying a decision on your mortgage application.

■ *CAUTION NOTE: A low down payment can often delay a mortgage application because of scrutiny of credit and property.*

HOW POINTS AFFECT AFFORDABILITY

As we have discussed, points are taken out when you originally get your loan. Each point equals 1% of the loan, which can be costly and become a determining factor in which loan you choose. For example, which $100,000 loan would you choose: 10% with 3 points, that is, $3,000, or 10¼% with 1½ points, or $1,500?

At first glance, it may seem that paying the extra point and a half to get the lower interest rate is the best deal, but if you plan on staying in the property for only a few years, it will take a lot of extra monthly payments to equal the $1,500 cost of additional points. However, if you need to minimize monthly payments to qualify for a mortgage, it may be wise for you to pay all three points up front to get the lower rate.

■ *CAUTION NOTE: Points, like other closing costs, require several years to pay back.*

HOW VARIABLE RATES PLAY HAVOC WITH YOUR BUDGET

One of the many reasons you must be careful in choosing an ARM is that you are then subject to the ups and downs of interest rates, and it is the ups that can raise havoc with your monthly budget. As you can see by the Affordability Chart in Figure 3.1, a rise of two points in interest over the course of the year can make astronomical jumps in your monthly mortgage payment. What starts out as 8 or 8½% can often be a point and a half or two points higher within a year, perhaps in three or four years capping out at 5 or 6% higher, depending on the specific terms of your loan.

■ *CAUTION NOTE: A variable rate sliding upward can cause a considerable rise in your monthly payment.*

It is true, however, that the uncertainty of higher rates in the future is somewhat balanced out by lower initial rates that give you some rate hike protection in the early years. You just have to be prepared to pay higher rates in the future, and if you are planning on being in the house for a short period of time, this may be the wisest course.

■ *KEY POINT:　A higher rate in the future is often balanced by a lower initial rate.*

These are comparisons you must make with the mortgages available to you in your local marketplace. Compare, for example, an 11%, fixed rate mortgage; a one-year ARM at 8½% with a 2% interest rate cap in any given year and a 5-point cap over the life of the loan; and a three-year ARM at 10 percent with the same 2–5 caps. In the worst situation, the one-year ARM will rise to 10½% after year one, to 12½% after year two (making it more expensive than the fixed rate mortgage), and to 13½%—the maximum allowed—in the next year. The three-year ARM, in contrast, isn't adjusted for the extra two percentage points to 12% until after year three. You only beat the fixed rate loan for a short period on both, and only for an extra year on the three-year ARM.

Worst case mortgage comparison			
	Fixed-Rate Mortgage	One-Year ARM	Three-Year ARM
First Year	11%	8½%	10%
Second Year	11%	10½%	10%
Third Year	11%	12½%	12%
Fourth Year	11%	13½% (Maximum allowed)	14%

Underlying this whole discussion, particularly regarding adjustable rate loans, is that it is impossible to predict where these loans are going, whether they will rise or fall. What you must hope for if you choose an ARM, is that rates will remain stable and that your initial lower ARM rate will stay low.

■ *CAUTION NOTE: Caution is required for ARMs because of the unpredictable nature of varying interest rates.*

One recommendation is to consider convertible ARMs, which allow you to switch from an adjustable rate to a fixed rate mortgage. At similar cost it is wise to choose the convertible ARM in case interest rates skyrocket. However, there are fees for converting to a fixed rate loan if you do decide to change, and you must analyze the final financial impact of doing so.

■ *KEY POINT: Consider an ARM that allows conversion to a conventional loan.*

CHOOSING THE RIGHT MORTGAGE

4

The common problem in financing your real estate purchase is not finding the mortgage but choosing the best mortgage among several competing choices. Unlike a decade ago, now there are many lenders and banking institutions competing for your business. There are many things to choose from. Interest rates, the monthly payments you can afford, the term in which the loan will be negotiated, and the points to originate a loan, as well as the prepayment points for paying off a loan before its maturity, are among the several factors you need to consider in choosing the right loan.

■ *KEY POINT:* *Many lenders compete for your business.*

The key is to work within your financial bounds, that is, what you can best afford now and in the future. For many of us, that means squeezing into a loan in the beginning, even stretching our ability to make monthly payments, so that in the future, with possible rising income, we can settle in comfortably to our payment schedule.

■ *KEY POINT:* *Sometimes we must anticipate future income to comfortably meet our loan schedule.*

If you lack cash to put down on a property and have to make a minimal down payment, you increase the amount of money you pay monthly. That difference must be made up in the amount of income you receive. If you have owned a house before or have some cash, or if you are able to get help from your family to make a larger down payment, your mortgage and therefore your monthly payments will not be as high and will fit better into your financial structure.

■ *KEY POINT: A higher down payment means a smaller mortgage and thus smaller monthly payments.*

Most people today still choose a conventional mortgage, that is, one with a fixed rate of interest over a 25- or 30-year term, that is self-amortizing, with 10 or 15% down and constant, equal monthly payments. Many of the other loans you consider, such as adjustable rate mortgages, you will want to compare with the conventional mortgage.

■ *KEY POINT: Most borrowers opt for a steady-rate, self-amortizing conventional loan that requires a modest amount down.*

As you have seen in this book, the rates for some types of variable interest loans start below the average conventional rate, but may rise to a higher percentage than the fixed rate later on.

■ *CAUTION NOTE: Avoid a variable rate that could escalate unreasonably.*

SHOPPING FOR A MORTGAGE

Here are some major points to consider in choosing available mortgage alternatives.

Type of Loan: Fixed Rate or Adjustable?

Do you get a fixed rate or an adjustable rate mortgage? Certainty comes with a fixed rate loan because you pay the same amount to your lender every month. With the adjustable rate mortgage, although the interest rate can initially be lower, it can rise and fall during the term of the mortgage. It normally starts off at a lower rate, such as 1½ or 2 points below that for fixed mortgages, and it does have limits, such as no more than a 2-point rise over the course of a year, or 5 or 6 percentage points over the term of the mortgage.

■ *CAUTION NOTES: Make sure adjustable loans contain limits on rate rises.*

Even one or two percentage points on a mortgage can affect your monthly payments.

ARMs are attractive if you plan to sell a house in three or four years; that way you are not likely to get stuck with the 2% to 4% increase your monthly payments will probably be calculated on in a few years. It depends a lot on the difference between the starting interest rate with an ARM and what is charged for a conventional loan. If an adjustable rate mortgage is two and a half or three points lower than a fixed rate mortgage, it may be wise for you to consider this. You can often convert this loan to a fixed rate loan in the future, even if you have to go to another lending institution.

■ *KEY POINT: With an ARM there is always the possibility of future conversion or renegotiation.*

Another factor in deciding on an ARM loan is your expectations for your future income: Will it rise dramatically within a few years? If you are on a low budget but in a job where your income will advance as you advance, the lower rate now may be something to consider. If you are on a more fixed income and don't see any excess cash in the future, now may be the time for you to lock in that fixed rate.

Term of Loan: Short or Long?

Shorter loans have been desirable in recent years as moderate rates have allowed borrowers to afford the payments demanded by a more rapid payoff schedule.

An obvious advantage is the substantial amount of money to be saved in interest over the term of the mortgage. For example, an $80,000 loan with a 9½%, 25-year term has monthly payments of $699; with a 9%, 15-year loan (you usually get a slightly lower interest rate for choosing a shorter-term loan) the payment is $811 a month.

Even though it costs $112 more a month, total payments on the shorter loan would be $63,720 less over the life of the loan, compared with the 25-year term. If you are keeping the house over the term of its loan, you can see that the short term might be wise. Even if you sell within a few years, the 15-year loan has paid off equity at a more rapid rate. Over the first 6 years, for example, you would have paid an extra $8,064 on the 15-year mortgage but accumulated $13,706 more equity (principal paid off) than with the 25-year loan.

■ *KEY POINT:*   *Shorter-term loans mean more rapid principal payoff.*

The other side of the coin in negotiating a short-term loan is that, although you save interest expense, you must consider what the money spent on the higher payments can earn elsewhere. Payments are approximately 20 to 25% higher on a 30-year loan than on a 15-year loan. That in itself is a substantial difference, but consider what other opportunities you might be able to pursue with that extra money over the course of the loan. For example, the difference of $112 in the monthly payment illustrated in the last example, if invested at 10% over 6 years, would grow to $10,988—comparable to the savings in principal payoff!

■ *CAUTION NOTE:* *Rapid principal payoff in a shorter-term loan must be balanced against growth earned by your money elsewhere.*

Granted, some of us need the discipline of a forced savings plan, but if you took the amount you saved each month on the lower payments of the longer-term loan and put them into an investment that yielded more than the interest on your mortgage, you could have substantially more money over the full term of the mortgage, plus you would have money at your immediate disposal should you need it for a major expenditure.

In conclusion, it is often hard to say whether a 15- or 20-year loan is better than a 25- or 30-year loan. Often with a shorter-term loan, you can negotiate a lower interest rate, but as you have read here, sometimes you can make a wiser investment than the cost of your mortgage with the extra monthly money this loan requires. A 15-year, $75,000 mortgage costs about $850 a month, versus $715 for the 30-year loan—a difference of approximately 16% in higher monthly costs. With the shorter-term loan, however, it is possible for the rate to be a quarter to two-thirds less than on the longer-term mortgage. And for the length of the term, you will cut your interest charges approximately in half.

■ *KEY POINT:* *The decision on short or long term is often one of personal preference.*

You also have to remember that mortgage interest is tax-deductible, and the extra interest you pay on a longer-term loan is at least deductible, if somewhat diminished, under the lower tax rate of the new tax code.

With a short-term loan, shelling out more dollars but paying less interest swells your monthly costs, in contrast to the lower payments of the 30-year loan that may allow you to afford a more substantial or more suitable home. If you take out the shorter-term mortgage, you are locked into higher payments and committed to an investment yielding whatever that mortgage rate is. As other opportunities at higher rates come your way over the years, you may not have this extra money to invest.

■ *KEY POINT: The lower payments of a longer-term loan may allow you to afford a more substantial house.*

For those who choose longer payment plans, there is always the opportunity of accelerating payments. You can even add a set amount to each monthly payment, essentially creating your own mortgage plan and thus effectively shortening the term of your long-term loan. You may even wish to send your lender a lump sum amount at the end of the year, should you come into extra money. These additional monies are applied against the principal, thereby shortening the term of the loan and decreasing the amount of interest you will pay.

■ *KEY POINT: Most mortgage balances can be brought down with extra payments made at your convenience.*

The key thing is, if you have something better to do with your extra money—and have the proper discipline—you can often save at a higher rate of interest than your present mortgage interest rate. Overall, the better investment opportunity is the one with the higher interest. This doesn't mean that choosing the shorter term may not be advantageous for you. It depends on what your income is, how long you intend to live in the home, and whether you are a wise investor. There are advantages to both short-term and long-term loans.

■ *CAUTION NOTE: Discipline is required to make regular payments to an investment plan designed to take advantage of mortgage payments.*

■ *Further note: If alterntive rates of investment are less than the interest rate on your mortgage, you may be wise to invest at the rate of your mortgage, specifically by paying off a portion of your mortgage balance. In this way you are decreasing a committed higher rate instead of earning less at a lower rate. You can do this by adding to your monthly payments or making lump sum payments against the outstanding balance.*

Cost of Property: Large or Small Mortgage

Obvious, but often unstated, is the fact that the cost of the house determines, to a large degree, the size of the mortgage needed to finance it. Whether you are putting down a minimum of 5% or a more substantial 20%, the size of the mortgage does not trail far behind the purchase price.

■ *KEY POINT: The purchase price sets the size of the mortgage.*

Do not buy just what you can afford, or feel obligated to buy the most expensive house you can borrow money on. Spend only what you feel comfortable with, always giving yourself a cushion of as much money as possible for unexpected maintenance or capital expenditures, as well as family emergencies.

■ *KEY POINT: Purchase in the range you can afford.*

Rate of Interest

When you read in the paper about mortgage rates rising and falling, it may seem like they all move in one concerted mass. In general, within regions throughout the country, rates do tend to move in lockstep, as they are often controlled by national financial policy.

But rates offered by banks in your local area can often vary a percentage point, so it is wise to shop around. Perhaps there are weekly mortgage comparisons published locally. Your agent can keep you informed, and there are services that offer research on current mortgage costs.

■ *KEY POINT: Shop local lenders for the best interest rate.*

There is often a connection between interest rates and prices of real estate. In some "hot" regions, people don't care about price, as long as they can find favorable financing, especially at rates that look like bargains. Conversely, a higher interest rate often translates into lower property prices. Real estate prices also may vary with the availability or scarcity of mortgage money, a beneficial point if, with your mortgage proposal, you can edge out fellow mortgage seekers for that scarce money and thus be able to buy at a comparatively lower price. All in all, be aware that current conditions in both the real estate and mortgage markets affect the lender's willingness to negotiate on rates.

A variety of mortgages and rates are available to you at any one time. The rates in the chart in Figure 4.1 are averages that we have seen in recent years. You will have to check your local lending institutions for the precise rates being charged at any given time.

The chart is intended only to show you the differences between rates for various types of loans, as well as the points and amount of interest charged. The amounts are based on a loan of $120,000. Down payments range between 5 and 20%, with fewer points paid with the higher down payments.

COMPARE LOANS TO DECIDE
WHICH IS BEST

There is no single mortgage format that is ideal for all borrowers. You need to choose the financial strategy that works best for you. To make your decision easier, look at the amount of money you have for a down payment and your income level. Certainly, if you have plenty of money for a down payment and are married with a substantial combined income, you can afford most homes on the market.

But most people, particularly those negotiating a mortgage for their first property, have to squeeze into the best property they can afford. They have to minimize the down payment requirement and skirt the edge of 28 to 30% of their gross annual income in calculating affordable mortgage payments and insurance and taxes.

Many varieties of mortgage exist and because of people's varied requirements, that is a boon. Two factors of particular interest to most people are interest rate, for example, variable interest on the adjustable rate mortgages, and the term on which the loan is based.

■ *KEY POINT:* *There are many varieties of mortgage format from which to choose.*

Too many people automatically go for the 30-year mortgage, but as you can see from the tables in this chapter, a 30-year mortgage pays a great deal more interest than does a 15- or 20-year mortgage. People who think they are going to move within 4 or 5 years may not care a great deal about the term, because if they don't pay off much principal, they will increase their equity greatly, simply by the value of their property increasing. This is one factor that depends on whether you will be staying in your new home or moving on in a few years.

■ *KEY POINT:* *Staying in a property for only a few years affects the choice of mortgage.*

But if you are buying to settle down in an area, you may very well want to look at the 15- or 20-year mortgage with an eye to

(Note: Rates show average differences between types of loans rather than current rates)

Type	Rate	Minimum Down	Recommended Down	Points	Monthly Payment	Total Interest Cost
30-year fixed	9–12%	5%	20%	0–4%	$966–1,234	$227,700–324,360
Remarks: Popular with first-time borrowers. Higher interest payments made over longer term. Fixed rate stabilizes interest.						
25-year fixed	8.5–11.5%	5%	20%	0–4%	$966–1,220	$227,700–246,000
Remarks: Fixed rate offers protection from increases. Slightly lower rate means less interest paid but higher monthly payment.						
20-year fixed	8.5–11.5%	5%	20%	0–4%	$1,080–1,280	$139,100–187,100
Remarks: Most popular until go-go age of 1970s. Still most balanced in interest paid and length of term.						
15-year fixed	8–11%	5%	20%	0–4%	$1,147–1,364	$86,420–125,500
Remarks: Shortest term generally available. Highest payments but less interest paid overall.						
Minimal Credit	9.5–12.5%	20%	20%	2–5%	$1,119–1,363	$148,600–207,200
Remarks: Higher interest rate and more down for low-credit borrower. Higher payments and points result.						

	Rate			Points	Payment	Price Range
Strong Credit High Down	8–11%	20%	25%	1–3%	$1,004–1,239	$120,900–177,300

Remarks: More down means lower interest rate and points.

Bi-weekly Payment	9.25–10.5%	5%	20%	1–3%	$823–915	$131,900–143,500

Remarks: 26 payments per year. Excellent loan for negotiating low rate and points. Less interest over term. Extra payments require high income.

7-year Balloon	8.5–11%	5%	20%	1–4%	$923–1,143	$69,200–90,600

Remarks: Lower payments and rate, but payoff in short term may require selling or refinancing. Possibly interest only.

10-Year Balloon	8.5–11%	5%	20%	1–4%	$923–1,143	$97,000–127,800

Remarks: Same as 7-year balloon but longer time to negotiate payoff.

One-year Adjustable	7–10.5%	5%	20%	0–3.5%	$798–1,097	variable

Remarks: Lower promotional rate and possibly no points going in, but subject to uncertainty of future rate increases, particularly after first year.

Three-year Adjustable	8–11%	5%	20%	1–3.5%	$880–1,143	variable

Remarks: As with one-year adjustable above, lower beginning rate and points. With both, negotiate caps on yearly and life-of-loan interest rises. Good loans in higher interest periods for those who plan to sell in a short time.

Figure 4.1 Guide through the mortgage market.

minimizing your overall interest. You can also look at the shorter-term mortgage as an enforced savings plan, in that you are paying more per month, but in 15 or 20 years you can have a mortgage burning party. So reducing the term to lower overall interest costs or reducing or extending monthly payments, making a lower or higher down payment, and negotiating points or interest rates are all alternatives that can make the terms of a mortgage more suitable to you.

Not all banks offer every alternative discussed in this book. In fact, many of the new techniques that you read about in monthly periodicals never become a reality in local mortgage markets, where the choices must be made. But the basic types of conventional loans—fixed rate, adjustable rate, adjustable rate and fixed rate loans with balloon payments, and convertible loans—are generally available at most lending institutions.

The best loan for you is one that meets your particular needs and circumstances, allowing you to purchase the property. That is the key thing: to get a property you can afford. The loan is merely a financial tool with which you can purchase real estate. It is there to help you make up the difference between the down payment you can comfortably put down and the purchase price of the property.

■ *KEY POINT: A mortgage loan is merely a financial tool to purchase property, which you structure to pay back in a way that most logically meets your needs.*

GUIDELINES FOR COMPARING LOANS

Here are some guidelines you can use to compare different loans.

How Much Down Payment Are You Required to Put Down?

The larger the mortgage you have, the higher your obligations, specifically the monthly payment you will make, are likely to be. Generally, the interest rate for a 5% loan is higher than the rate for a loan in which you can put at least 20% down.

Occasionally, banks will even give you a special deal if you can put 30% down. You can't put a great deal of money down unless you have owned a property before or have spent years saving money, so in putting a relatively small 5 or 10% down, you need to look at the terms of the mortgage and structure them so that you can afford them.

Is the Interest Rate Fixed or Variable?

Will the rate be fixed or will it change during the term of the loan, thereby affecting your monthly payments? Are these changes scheduled at certain planned times, or will they happen on a random basis—for example, variable rate financing, where the interest rate is tied to some national figure such as the prime rate?

Is it possible for you to keep the same interest rate but have graduated payments, perhaps lower in the beginning and rising later on as your income increases?

How Much Can an Adjustable Rate Change?

What are the limits on how much the interest rate on an adjustable rate loan can increase each year, as well as over the term of the loan? A point and a half or two points should be the maximum increase each year, with a 5 or 6% cap over the term of the loan. Whatever the limits, be sure to negotiate the lowest possible interest rate in the beginning.

Can You Convert to a Fixed-Term Loan Later On?

Is it possible for you to convert an adjustable rate loan to a fixed rate loan later on if interest rates stabilize? Often adjustable rate loans will have this convertibility option.

Can You Extend the Life of a Shorter-Term Loan?

If you do negotiate a shorter-term loan, is it possible to extend the term later on? In addition, if you negotiate a balloon payment to pay off the principal balance of the loan in five or ten years, can you extend with that same bank at the then-current interest rate, without new title search and other costs?

What Index Is Used to Compute the Adjustable Rate?

In adjustable rate loans, what is the index used to compute the interest rate? You do not want to agree to a volatile index, such as the consumer price index, that may rise and fall continually. It should be a national indicator that moves slowly.

What About Prepayment Penalties?

Is there a prepayment penalty if you pay off your 25- or 30-year loan before the end of the term? You may wish to sell your property 5 or 10 years after purchase because of a transfer or a job change. Are you going to be penalized one, two, or three points at that time? Often mortgage lenders will want to have a prepayment clause in the mortgage contract.

What you need to do as a borrower is minimize the points or at least negotiate a time limit of four or five years in which the prepayment penalty would be in effect.

Can Your Loan Be Assumed?

Can the loan be assumed by a qualified purchaser, one to whom you may wish to sell your property? Most banks have prohibitions in the mortgage contract against this possibility. However, if they are satisfied with the interest rate and they have a qualified purchaser, it's not to their disadvantage to accept a new signer on the loan. They may require you to remain on the loan, but the equity position of the loan balance several years down the road makes both your position and the bank's very secure.

Are There Any Unfamiliar Tax Consequences?

Are there any new roles in the tax law specifically regarding the deductibility of interest that may adversely affect you? Speak to your local CPA or tax attorney for advice in this area.

Will You Always Be Able to Afford the Loan?

Finally, consider not only the loan that is going to get you into the house, but the one you can live with for a long period of time, one whose cost, if variable, is going to rise less than your income rises.

SIX POINTS ON CHOOSING A MORTGAGE

First, seek out a loan with the lowest possible interest cost. Among the many terms and conditions you will negotiate in a mortgage loan, interest is the most important because of its inherent cost, which can be considerable over a period of time. The interest amount may be the same on two different types of loans, but the overall interest cost over a period of time may be less on a loan ending in 25 years than one ending in 30 years. Sometimes the way in which a loan is paid off, such as bi-weekly payments, can further minimize interest over a period of time.

Second, make sure that the mortgage's total cost for the monthly or bi-weekly period in which you will pay it, including any points or additional fees that start the loan or mortgage insurance premiums, is one you can afford, and will continue to be able to afford even though the payments may change in the future.

Third, compare the mortgage to other investment choices. What alternatives are there? Is it best for you to minimize the down payment, get a larger mortgage, and invest the extra cash you may have? Alternatively, will the rate you invest at be lower than the rate you have to pay for the mortgage, so that having less mortgage becomes the wisest investment?

Fourth, reduce overall interest costs and the principal balance of your mortgage by making as substantial a down payment as possible. Again, you have to measure a large down payment against alternative investments. It may be wise for you to put a minimal amount down in order to gain more financial strength elsewhere.

Fifth, be on the lookout for restructuring opportunities. Financing should not be viewed as something that must remain unchanged from the time the property is first bought. There are always opportunities to refinance or restructure loans. If the interest rates are fairly high when you get your loan and then drop dramatically a few years later, you will want to restructure your loan with your present lender or pay the loan off with a new loan from another lender at the lower rate. You must always be flexible to take care of any change in the economic environment.

Sixth, do not burden yourself financially. Your down payment, upfront closing costs, and interest rate must be affordable and in concert with a financial plan that meets your individual needs.

WHERE DO YOU GET YOUR MORTGAGE MONEY? 5

Banks loan most of the mortgages given out in the United States. Many of us think a bank is the only source of financing. However, there are other options that are often less expensive and more flexible. Some of the best sources may be those that take a little creative planning. In this chapter we will review some of the many different sources of financing and what kinds of mortgages are offered.

WHOM DO YOU ASK FOR YOUR MORTGAGE? FROM BANKERS TO SELLERS

Mortgage money is available from so many different sources that it can make the selection downright confusing. Innumerable types of banks from savings and loans to commercial banks to credit unions stand ready to lend you money.

To choose the best one that will keep your mortgage costs down, you need to become familiar with some of the different possibilities. Thousands of dollars can be saved over the life of a mortgage by just negotiating at a lower interest rate. And, as we saw in the last chapter, having to pay points just for the privilege of being loaned money can hit hard financially.

■ *KEY POINT:*   *The variety of loan sources helps hold down costs.*

As you'll see here, there are a multitude of ways to negotiate low-cost loans.

SEVEN SOURCES FOR MONEY AND HOW TO APPROACH EACH

Seller Financing.   The best source of financing is the person from whom you buy the property. Often overlooked, the seller is motivated to make a deal. More times than not, this seller will help you finance. And it's not hard to negotiate. All you have to do is make your offer contingent on the seller's providing a specific amount of financing. It could be the full first mortgage at a fixed rate or assuming his or her loan with a second mortgage to help you with the down payment.

■ *KEY POINT:*   *Sellers often help with financing.*

Often you negotiate a better interest rate than with a bank. If you're dealing with a real estate agent, he or she may discourage you from asking the seller for help. After all, agents are bound by law to work for the seller. Even agents are surprised at how frequently sellers are willing to help.

■ *KEY POINT:*   *You can get a better interest rate from a seller.*

The seller's greatest motivation may be to get out, and if he has to help finance he will. An added benefit for him is that he can defer some of his taxable gain over a period of time. For example, if the seller gives a buyer an eight-year mortgage on 90% of the property's value, the seller can spread the profits of the sale over each one of those eight years, that is, he does not have to declare a lump-sum profit that would be taxed at a much higher rate.

■ *KEY POINT: When the seller gives the loan, he can save taxes.*

Savings Banks.   Savings banks, which are called by different names in each region of the country, make the majority of residential loans in the United States. These banks are usually in each community and mortgage officers are active in selling their money to you. They make home and investment loans.

■ *KEY POINT: Savings banks loan the most mortgage money.*

Savings banks are one of the easiest institutions to approach. Go and chat with them before you start looking for property. Ask them about availability of money, current interest rates, and the types of properties they give mortgages for. If you establish a rapport with a mortgage officer before you buy, it will make the actual commitment much easier and quicker to get once you find the property.

■ *KEY POINT: Savings banks are prepared to act fast.*

Mutual Savings Banks.   A major source of mortgage money is the mutual savings bank. Like savings banks, they may be called by a variety of names in different areas of the country. Mutuals, savings banks, and cooperative banks all have a distinction that separates them from some of their more commercial competitors: they are owned by the depositors. They are not corporations with stockholding owners. They operate as large joint ventures or partnerships similar to cooperatives. They are like the New England town meeting. Depositors have a say in who the directors of the bank are and encourage good public relations for the bank in their community.

■ *KEY POINT: Mutual savings banks are like cooperatives, and they will work with you if you deposit funds with them.*

These banks tend to be small, although many have become large by merging with other banks. They, like true savings and loans (S&L), have offices that are easily accessible and mortgage officers anxious to place their money in the community. As with savings and loans, they're easy to approach. However, they often require you to open a savings account for a nominal amount in order to be eligible for a loan.

Commercial Banks.   Commercial banks, in their desire to expand beyond checking accounts and business and car loans, have steadily moved into the mortgage market. They tend to be more conservative than savings banks, but many borrowers have found them to be excellent sources for larger amounts of money, particularly those making larger investments. They also make residential loans. If you need an extra $25,000 or $40,000 to fix up a house, they are the place to go.

■ *KEY POINT: Commercial banks aggressively loan for home improvements and, increasingly, mortgages.*

Commercial banks, perhaps due to their history of loaning money to business, are often more likely than savings banks to loan money beyond the initial mortgage to finance a two-car garage or mother-in-law apartment.

You approach them as you would the other banks, with information about the property and your financial circumstances. You can negotiate interest rate and terms, but be aware that they have more of a need than other banks for profitability. They're stockholder-owned corporations that seek a return on invested capital. This often makes their interest rate slightly higher than the mutual or cooperatively owned banks. Although they must be competitive, they are one of the more versatile sources of mortgage funds. Perhaps their experience in dealing with business owners for many years has made them flexible to varying the terms and conditions of a loan.

■ *KEY POINT: Commercial banks can be approached for personal loans and second mortgages.*

Mortgage Brokers. Mortgage brokers are a cross between an institution and an individual. They don't usually have large, banklike buildings; more often they're located in an office storefront. What the mortgage broker does is originate a loan with money he or she has usually borrowed from a commercial source, which he or she in turn sells to a large institutional investor such as an insurance company.

These bankers broker mortgages. That is, they do all the origination work for a fee. They usually place large loans on investment property, apartments, condominiums, and commercial stores.

■ *KEY POINT: The mortgage broker acts as a go-between with large banks for investment loans.*

They are not always a good source for home loans. They usually prefer large deals, and their rates are not always competitive. They usually charge an extra percent or two beyond the normal cost of money to include their fee.

Mortgage brokers are also fond of charging points, and after dealing with them you may feel they want to make it as hard as possible for you to negotiate a loan. However, for certain types of projects that may be beyond the scope of your local savings bank, they can be an efficient source, since they can cut red tape to a minimum, ensuring you a quick commitment.

■ *CAUTION NOTE: Mortgage brokers often charge high fees for their service.*

Credit Unions. Credit unions can be your best source of mortgage money if you are a member or eligible to be one. Credit unions are often established for employees of a large business or university. They're like a miniature bank run for the benefit of their employee members.

Large companies such as General Motors and IBM, most state universities, and even government entities have credit unions which members can turn to for personal loans or mortgage money. They aren't as experienced in placing mortgages as full-fledged mortgage or savings banks, but this can work to your advantage. Any information you can give them on the value of the property and your own economic resources goes a long way in gaining a favorable decision, as credit unions don't usually have the capability to do the research themselves.

■ *KEY POINT: If you're a member, a credit union is an excellent source for a reasonably priced loan.*

Insurance Companies and Pension Funds. Two other sources of money remain: insurance companies and pension funds. They usually loan money on investment projects, that is, $500,000 and up. In fact, they're almost the sole source of money for projects of several million or more.

It's possible but rare to get a mortgage commitment from either in less than several weeks. The necessary paperwork and the formal appraisal work involved in granting mortgage money of this magnitude takes time. Careful calculations ensure the insurance company or pension fund is secure in the investment. All of this documentation is time-consuming.

■ *KEY POINT: Insurance companies and pension funds often loan large amounts under complex arrangements.*

Your proposal and the work involved in the lender's decision-making are not different from the process described in Chapter

1, just larger in magnitude. A loan officer or investment committee can give overnight approval. Numerous people in different levels of management are involved in approving these loans. The step-by-step way in which a loan is considered by an insurance company is the same as getting a mortgage from your local S&L.

A group of investors must have detailed architect's plans and innumerable financial projections made by computer, including building and zoning approval from local authorities, all of which are required when major decisions are made.

Most insurance companies that place loans of this type have real estate departments or someone appointed in your region acting for them. Fees are charged for the preliminary investigation by the insurance company or trust fund. Although these fees alone may be thousands of dollars, they make the complicated loan process move forward and are evidence to the insurance company or fund of the seriousness of your intentions.

■ *CAUTION NOTE:* *Insurance companies often charge heavy fees up-front to negotiate loans with them.*

The insurance company is in the business of lending money; approach it with the help of competent attorneys, architects, and builders.

HOW TO SELECT THE BEST MONEY SOURCE

Not all of the seven sources for mortgage money may be in your community. However, you may have one or two savings banks and a commercial bank, perhaps even a credit union where you work. You may be in a small community where there's only one source or in a suburb of a large city that has innumerable banks of each description.

The best way to select a source for a mortgage is to become familiar with each before you find the property you wish to purchase. This way you don't narrow down your choice to a single institution until you've checked the most favorable interest rates or terms. You establish contact with the different mortgage officers. It is their job to help you; more important, they can often take your side and support your needs, influencing those in the bank who make the decisions.

It is important to develop an ongoing relationship with a banker. It is appropriate to take him or her to lunch, make him or her familiar with you and your finances. Loan officers like people who come to them prepared and who think ahead enough to make their job easier—these are most often the people who are never late with payments.

■ *CAUTION NOTE: Don't deal with just one institution until you investigate the mortgage plans in all.*

■ *KEY POINT: Personal contact with an individual banker is critical for negotiations.*

Sometimes you cannot always do this preliminary work. If you are coming in from out of town on a weekend looking for a new house, you'll likely spend most of your time looking at the real estate advertisements. You'll probably be tied up with real estate agents. Still, try and visit a bank or two. If you cannot, get as much information as you can from the agents or even sellers about what's happening in the local mortgage market.

This extra time stops you from rushing the decision. Shop for both the right property and rates. Now is the time you can be assembling the information to make a valid comparison of loans on the basis of rate, points and terms.

■ *KEY POINT: When viewing property in a new area, visit banks too.*

When you look at a house, find out where the existing loan is placed. Next to the seller himself, the bank that has the money invested in the property is often the best source. Since a portion of the money needed for a new mortgage is already placed on the property and the bank often needs to add a little more to get a slightly higher interest rate on the whole amount, they are anxious to do business. In fact, they are often flexible enough to reduce or even eliminate points.

■ *KEY POINT: The bank that holds the existing financing is the best possibility for new money.*

Now, in the next few chapters let's look at types of mortgages and where you go to get them. It is not only knowledge of the source but the way in which the financing itself is constructed that will lead you to make the best decision and negotiate the best deal in a mortgage program.

GETTING CREATIVE WITH CONVENTIONAL FINANCING 6

When you need financing to buy a home or an income property, institutional lenders stand ready to loan you what you need. Mortgage officers, who are easy to approach and who are skilled at making loans, are prepared, within the parameters of a bank's lending policy, to help you.

The loan itself, however, is an entirely other matter, and in this chapter you will find out how to put your best foot forward in getting a conventional loan—what you can do to smooth the way and get a favorable decision.

THE FIRST CHOICE: DO YOU WANT TO GAMBLE ON INTEREST RATES?

First, do you want the conventional fixed rate loan? After all, most banks also give adjustable rate loans. In the ARM, the monthly payments vary according to a changing interest rate dependent upon overall economic indices; by contrast, the fixed rate loan is based on a constant rate of interest negotiated at the time the loan is made.

■ *KEY POINT: Choosing between a fixed rate mortgage and an ARM is a major decision when dealing with the bank.*

Usually adjustable loans are reviewed every quarter or six months, and, based on some national economic index like the consumer price index (CPI), may move downward or upward. If the interest rate moves upward in an adjustable rate mortgage, you may have to face a higher monthly payment, as the bank sets its new interest rate on your loan.

■ *CAUTION NOTE: Over time, the rate in an ARM is likely to move upward.*

If you wish to gamble that interest rates will fall, the adjustable rate loan, often starting a point or so below average rates, may be your best bet. It may fall even further.

If you feel interest rates are going to increase, you may choose a fixed rate loan. It may be a point or so higher than the adjustable rate, but it will remain at the negotiated interest rate until you sell your property, pay off the loan, or refinance it.

■ *KEY POINT: Fixed rate loans are better when you expect average rates to increase.*

The future of interest rates is not the only factor in the decision. More important is to consider the advantages of a fixed rate loan. You may desire the predictability of a constant payment for your monthly budget.

The stability of the payment can be a benefit. As times goes on, the money you earn makes these payments seem smaller in size. Since the value of the dollar declines over time—the dollar buys less each year—this, combined with your rising income, helps with the fixed payment.

■ *KEY POINT: The stability of the fixed payment may benefit you in the future.*

If you have an adjustable rate loan, a rising national rate may boost your interest rate, sometimes substantially higher than what you could have negotiated for a fixed rate loan when you originated the loan.

Of all the important things to concern yourself with in this world, the chance of your mortgage payment rising shouldn't be one of them.

Now, will rates go down? Perhaps, and we will talk more about this and the advantages of an adjustable rate loan in the next chapter.

WHEN THE CONVENTIONAL LOAN MAY BE BEST FOR YOU

A clear benefit of the fixed rate loan is its absolute stability and predictability. You know what your mortgage payments are and don't have to worry about any changes occurring in the future.

If interest rates decline, you may want to do as many others with a fixed rate loan do: simply renegotiate to a lower interest rate. This is essentially applying for a new loan. Often a bank will require an updated title search and new loan agreement; they may also charge points, either to satisfy the prepayment condition in the old loan, or simply to originate the "new" loan.

■ *KEY POINT: Fixed rate mortgages can be refinanced.*

At the time you decide to refinance you should weigh whether the lower interest rate, and hence lower monthly payment, is worth paying several thousand dollars in points.

■ *CAUTION NOTE: Banks often charge points on refinancing.*

Of the loans originated today, about half are fixed rate and half adjustable rate. We can't predict how this proportion may change; it is based on borrowers' perceptions of where the interest rate may go and the desire for banks to make one type of loan over the other.

However, if you want to negotiate a monthly payment that will fit into your budget without having to worry if it's going to increase, then the conventional loan may be the best for you.

SHOPPING FOR THE CONVENTIONAL LOAN

Shopping for the right loan entails two tasks. One is to gather all the technical information relating to the different banks, that is, the types of programs available, how much interest is to be charged, and what points are charged. The second is to get the right banker to do business with. Banks are not just huge institutions. Like most enterprises, they are composed of people. When you negotiate a mortgage loan, you talk with one individual—the same person with whom you will follow through all negotiations.

■ *KEY POINT: Loan shopping includes getting the right information and making personal contact with a banker.*

Getting a loan is not like going up to a teller and discussing the amount of your checking account. Much more information will pass back and forth. Make lists. They will help you throughout these negotiations.

If you are able to choose a bank and banker before you buy, all the better. If you have agreed to purchase the property and then have 10–20 days in which to secure financing, you need to be prepared.

Your first list can be the various banks that offer conventional fixed-rate mortgages. Note that they will probably also offer adjustable rate mortgages. When discussing the best financial arrangements, you should consider each.

■ *KEY POINT:* *Make a list of the mortgage banks in your area and what they offer.*

All mortgage banks offer conventional fixed rate loans. They advertise their loans and interest rates in the local newspapers. They're looking for your business. In some areas, newspapers even publish a weekly list showing what each bank is charging (eg, rates and points) that is a good starting place for comparisons. However, the best way to get this information is to call the banks themselves. It isn't secret and begins your contact with the bank.

You may have six or more banks on your list. Once you have selected the bank to approach, establish a rapport with one of the bank's mortgage officers.

To negotiate your way out of an expensive prepayment penalty, whether in selling or refinancing, it's nice not to have to do business with a stranger, but with someone who you know will integrate the bank's requirements with your needs.

■ *KEY POINT:* *The banker you work with should not be a stranger.*

SELECTING THE BEST BANKER

To find bankers eager to do business with you, you need only turn to the display advertising section of your local paper to see numerous offerings of interest rates and different mortgages from your local, friendly banker. They compete for your business just like the real estate agents. It's their job to sell you money.

How should you choose one? Begin by talking to the mortgage officers of several banks to see with whom you are most comfortable. In choosing a bank, remember that the lowest interest rate is not the only factor; other terms and conditions —such as points, assumability, and length of term—affect a mortgage's value and suitability to you.

You want a banker with whom you have rapport, someone who will listen and be receptive to your requirements. You are not just looking for a rapid decision by the bank, but also want a mortgage that has the lowest possible rate, a minimum of points, and no prepayment penalty.

■ *KEY POINT: Besides favorable rates and terms, you want a banker with whom you can negotiate.*

To do this you need to establish with the banker of your choice a minimum measure of trust and confidence. You start by getting out and meeting them.

■ *KEY POINT: Establish trust and confidence with the banker.*

Most banks in an area don't vary much in the interest rates they charge for a fixed rate loan. Unfortunately, they tend to know what the other charges. It may seem like price fixing, but it's not. All they do is read what their competitiors charge in the newspaper.

A word of caution. A difference of a half a point or even a full point shouldn't automatically make you run to the bank with the lower rate. Usually such differences in rates are made up in the charging of points.

■ *CAUTION NOTE: Beware of low interest rate alone—differences are usually made up in points.*

HOW TO NEGOTIATE DOWN PAYMENTS AND INTEREST RATES

When a bank gives a fixed rate loan, they often have determined the percent of a property's value that they will loan. For example, most banks readily give an 80% loan. This means that they expect you to put down the other 20% in cash. However, this is not always true, as we will shortly see. Normally, if the bank verifies the value of the property, they will loan you the 80% balance.

■ *KEY POINT:* *Most banks normally lend 80% mortgages.*

Banks have special programs where they will loan up to 90% and even 95% in some cases. Private and government mortgage insurance programs guarantee to the bank that the loan will be paid off in case of default.

■ *KEY POINT:* *With private loan guarantees, banks often lend up to 95%.*

In buying your first home or investment property, you may need to get as much money as possible from the bank. In your proposal you should stress the high value of the property and your strong economic circumstances and ability to pay.

A 90% loan usually has a quarter or half a point higher interest rate than the 80% loan. Because of its higher overall amount of money, payments are slightly higher. In your proposal emphasize the fact that you can make those higher payments.

■ *CAUTION NOTE:* *Higher interest rates usually accompany 90% loans.*

Interest rates tend to be fixed, but often you can reduce them by choosing different loan programs. As we've seen, the interest can vary depending on the amount of mortgage required from the bank. You need to weigh each situation. For example, you might get one loan at 12% but with a 4% prepayment penalty, which would affect sale of the property within the ten years following. Weigh this against a 13% loan with no penalties.

■ *KEY POINT:* *In some banks interest rates can be negotiated downward by offering points.*

Considering all other factors are equal, if you anticipate making a change in real estate four or five years down the road, perhaps due to some job consideration, you'd be better off taking the higher interest rate.

WHAT DO YOU DO WHEN THEY ASK FOR "POINTS"?

To us, consumer points are a big bugaboo. These extra percentage points, charged as a one-time fee, are objectionable and expensive. And, too often, they are requested in granting a fixed rate loan, but not for an ARM. The bank's justification for points is paperwork and overhead costs—but why one loan and not the other? The answer is that you're going to pay one way or the other.

■ *CAUTION NOTE: Points are usually requested only on fixed rate loans.*

The idea behind mortgage financing is that banks earn their profit on the interest rate they gain over time. Then why are points charged? Simple: it's the latest gimmick for profit above and beyond the interest rate. Maybe if they didn't have so many branch offices, they wouldn't feel so pressured.

■ *CAUTION NOTE: Points are charged out of the need for more profit and to pay for burdensome overhead.*

But the news is not all bad. Points, even more than interest rates, are negotiable. The points are discretionary policy. They are not mandated by law, and have nothing to do with the basic interest rate of the loan. They don't relate to the bank's cost of money as much as they do to ongoing overhead. The two or three points they charge as a one-time fee are small compared with the interest the bank earns over the life of the loan. But from the borrower's perspective, a huge fee to start seems large.

■ *KEY POINT:* *Points can be negotiated downward, depending upon what they are for.*

When loan shopping, ask exactly what these points are for. And what programs are available that don't charge them.

Specifically, the penalty of paying points when you refinance or sell in the future is a provision a bank can agree to dispense with. Many disappointed borrowers have found a few years down the road that it costs them thousands of dollars as a one-time charge just to get out of the loan or to refinance it.

■ *CAUTION NOTE:* *Always try to negotiate prepayment points out of your mortgage agreement.*

Now, if a bank will give you a substantially lower fixed rate if you pay some points up front, then it may be beneficial. Some banks will do this for you. For the lower interest rate, they may get an extra two or three percentage points.

■ *KEY POINT:* *For a considerably lower interest rate, it may be worth paying points.*

How points are charged, how many of them are charged, and what length of time they are applicable are all issues that must be negotiated at the beginning of the loan, before you decide on a loan and sign the mortgage agreement.

THE BENEFITS OF LESS RED TAPE

The best way to cut red tape is to detail facts about the property you wish to buy and your economic situation. Certainly each bank has its own application to fill out, but the information they request is superficial. It doesn't allow you to put the best foot forward in terms of you or the property.

Most borrowers rely totally on the bank's investigative powers, not only to research the property but to verify their personal financial situation. This assumes they know everything. Often they will surprise you as to what they don't know. Your proposal will fill in the gaps. It minimizes the need for some of this investigative work, reducing a burden of the bank.

■ *CAUTION NOTE: Banks are not research experts.*

Remember that banks are concerned with three things: the value of the property; your ability to pay the mortgage and what reserves you have; the profit in it for them. If the bank is assured of the first two and you don't try and get their loan at below market rates, they will feel it's a profitable loan.

■ *KEY POINT: A mortgage proposal cuts red tape and assures the bank of property value, your ability to pay, and the loan's profitability.*

Red tape, though depending upon the requirements of each bank, is cut as much as possible by gaining the confidence of a mortgage officer and providing a proposal detailing information on the property and your economic situation.

ASSUME THE EXISTING MORTGAGE

You don't always have to originate a fixed rate loan. Some are assumable, meaning you can take them over for the remaining term of the loan.

Most loans granted before the early 1980s were conventional fixed rate loans. Many of these mortgages can be assumed as long as it isn't specifically prohibited in the agreement.

■ *KEY POINT:* *Mortgages can be assumed unless the agreement specifically prohibits it.*

Any loan you might want to assume should be checked by your lawyer to determine if it can be taken over without being called, that is, cancelled so the balance must be immediately paid.

■ *CAUTION NOTE:* *Beware of non-assumption clauses in mortgage agreements.*

Many of these older loans don't trigger a payoff upon transfer. For many years, when interest rates were relatively stable (without dramatic swings in one direction from one year to another), banks allowed assumptions. They just simply overlooked them. They were mildly irritating. After all, why would someone take over an existing loan when they could borrow more at the same rate?

Today's rates are usually much higher than those stated in old loans. However, it's likely the balance of an existing loan will be substantially less than the price you will pay for the property.

■ *KEY POINT:* *Assumptions of loans have become more common as rates have risen.*

So if you do assume an existing loan, you will want the seller to help you with some additional financing, such as a second mortgage to make up the difference between the balance of the old loan and the down payment which you can put down.

■ *KEY POINT:* *The seller will often make up the difference when a mortgage is assumed.*

Your rate on the assumed mortgage is likely to be favorable enough that you can easily offer a tempting rate on the second mortgage to the seller. When you combine the rates of the two mortgages, you will still be paying considerably less than you would in paying for a new mortgage. You could even pay a bit more for the property because this lower interest rate makes your effective cost of the property less than it seems.

In some areas assumable loans have been specifically excluded in mortgage agreements. Therefore, it is difficult to find property with a loan you can take over. It depends on the local situation. But next to the seller giving total financing (as seen in Chapter 8), assuming an existing loan is one of the first steps you should consider in buying any property.

■ *KEY POINT: Always investigate the possibility of assuming the existing loan.*

Note that some lenders call loans "assumable," but reserve the right to renegotiate all the terms upon transfer. Be sure to check the original loan contract. Many states have enacted legislation in an attempt to eliminate this problem, but it still exists in some areas.

MAKE YOUR OWN DEAL

Interest rates are one of your main considerations in any loan, especially a fixed rate loan, where the interest rate will remain constant for years. One way you can drive down the rate is to limit the bank's exposure—the ratio of loan to sale price.

You can do this by putting down a larger down payment, such as 30–40%, thereby limiting the bank's investment to 60–70%. If you could put down 50% so the bank only invested another 50%, you could get the lowest interest rate possible.

■ *KEY POINT: Negotiate a lower interest rate by limiting the amount of mortgage.*

Another way for you to limit the bank's exposure, but without putting down a large down payment, is to negotiate a second

mortgage with the seller. This eats up some of the down payment. For example, if you put down 10% and got another 25%
as a second mortgage, that would leave 65% of the mortgage,
which you would need to get from the bank. To keep the payments low, the term of the second mortgage could run for as
many years as the first.

■ *KEY POINT: Combine a bank mortgage with seller financing for
low interest.*

In the bank's view, the property is strong security for the
loan.

Mortgages that are low in comparison to the property's value
are also the easiest to negotiate. They don't require as much inspection of either your circumstances or the property, since the
security for the loan is high. And the bank knows it's profitable.
The mortgage officers don't have to justify their investment in
the loan as much as they would normally have to do.

■ *KEY POINT: Mortgages with "lower exposure" for the bank are
easier to negotiate.*

Under these circumstances, the paperwork can be completed
much more quickly. Often, you can gain a commitment the
same day you present the request.

HOW TO NEGOTIATE THE BEST TERMS

Many people think you can't negotiate a conventional fixed
rate loan. They believe that since banks have been making these
loans for years and since there is nothing new about them, the
rate and terms are set. That isn't true.

The mortgage market today is extremely competitive. Even
the larger, more central banks compete with each other in lending smaller banks money at the lowest possible interest

rates—rates passed on to you. The stiff competition among banks makes it possible for you to negotiate the lowest rate. You can often minimize or altogether eliminate the points charged for the origination fee or prepayment penalties. Often the banks don't feel they can afford to push for this extra money.

■ *KEY POINT: Competition forces banks to negotiate on rates and points.*

The key is to survey all the possible mortgage sources. In this way you are most likely to find one or more lenders who are willing to give you a mortgage at a better rate and terms.

And keep negotiating. Your preliminary survey of the banks and getting to know mortgage officers before you actually proceed with the property purchase helps make your deal go through faster.

■ *KEY POINT: Negotiating with all sources is the best assurance of getting the best deal.*

Sometimes it helps to let a banker know you're talking to other bankers—gently playing one against the other. This is a delicate maneuver, as you don't want to offend them or otherwise jeopardize your relationship with them.

You never want to give bankers the impression that you're a wheeler-dealer. Even if you're buying an investment property, it's still best to be modest. When negotiating, make them feel that they have something special to offer and that's why you want to negotiate with them. It's the best way to get them to see your point of view and ultimately to come up with the best interest rate and terms.

■ *CAUTION NOTE: Don't upset the relationship of trust with a banker.*

WHAT YOUR BANKER CAN AND CANNOT DO

Bankers are in the business of making sound financial decisions. They can loan you a reasonable percent of a property's selling price within the general parameters that their individual bank or state banking board has established. The percent loan to sale price amount is generally a maximum of 90%, although there are certain loan programs that go up to 95%. Some government loans, like the FHA with a 3% down payment, are even higher.

It's customary for banks to loan between 80 and 90% of the sales price. They cannot loan you 100%. If you only have $5,000 to put down on a $100,000 property, they cannot in most cases loan you the other 95% unless they see the value of the property as substantially more than $100,000.

■ *CAUTION NOTE: Banks can never loan you the full value of a property.*

You are also limited in how much you can negotiate on interest. They cannot go below what they themselves pay for the money. And when they re-lend it to you, they must add an additional 2–4% to cover their overhead and profit. For example, if a bank uses its own funds and pays its depositors an average of 8%, it is likely to charge another 4% for overhead, resulting in a rate of 12%. However, if the bank must borrow the money from another bank at, for example, 10%, then the rate they're going to charge is 14%.

■ *CAUTION NOTE: Banks have a limit on how low their interest rates are.*

Negotiating for the best terms can only be done within certain limits. The bank is most likely to be flexible on the issue of points. The bank may reduce or eliminate those charged in the origination of the loan or forgive them should the property be refinanced or sold at a later time. Too many borrowers wait until later to negotiate these prepayment points. They should be handled at the origination of the loan.

■ *KEY POINT: Banks can be more flexible on points than on interest rate.*

Banks also have the discretionary power to allow you to assume a supposedly non-assumable loan. Many states are beginning to enact laws permitting the direct assumption of loans. Banks, in feeling this pressure, are in some cases allowing assumptions that they might not otherwise have agreed to. It is a matter of negotiating.

INSIDE TIPS ON CONVENTIONAL LOANS

The guidelines for getting a conventional loan involve common sense. First, see if you can take over an existing mortgage either by assuming it or taking "subject to," that is, simply taking over payments without assuming liability. Taking over an old loan should always be explored. It depends, of course, on whether the loan balance is large enough and the interest rate is low. If so, it can be well worth doing so, even if you have to put down a larger down payment and work out a second mortgage with the seller.

■ *KEY POINT: Always see if you can assume a mortgage first.*

If the mortgage you wish to take over has a "due on sale clause," it means that the bank, should you take over the property and change the name on the property's title, could demand full payment of the balance. They could even start foreclosure proceedings.

The way to avoid this is to negotiate with the bank beforehand. They may very well say no but surprise you by allowing it with reasonable modifications, such as an increase in the interest rate—not necessarily to the full current rate but to a rate in between.

With an assumed loan, a relatively short term may remain. You may want to extend a 15-year balance, for example, to 25 years to make the monthly payments lower.

A smart borrower has the preliminary negotiations out of the way before committing to buy a particular property. Always done by professional investors, it also greatly benefits those making an occasional purchase of a house or investment property.

The key to getting the best interest rate and terms lies in the personal contact you have with a mortgage officer. This can be even more important than the actual bank with which you are going to do business.

■ *KEY POINT: Negotiate with a mortgage officer before you buy.*

The proposal you make up—information on the property and your own financial status and ability to pay and a cover letter that recognizes the need for the lender to profit from the arrangement—combined with a working relationship with a mortgage officer—goes a long way in getting a favorable and rapid commitment.

■ *KEY POINT: A mortgage proposal is the best way to get a favorable and quick commitment from the bank.*

Occasionally you will come across a property, usually a new one in a development, that a particular bank (in conjunction with the builder) is offering a "special" low interest rate on.

The rate may be four or five points lower than normal. Be wary of these loans. Generally, any interest rate you pay is based on a fair and common economic rationale for all parties concerned, and the bank will compensate for it in other ways. For example, if an 8% rate is offered when average conventional rates are hovering around 14%, often the difference is made up in the sales price. The arrangement works for the bank because the builder kicks back a big fee for each loan they give at the lower rate. Illegal? Not at all, as long as the deal is disclosed, even if only at closing; then it's too late to start complaining. Are you disadvantaged by this lower rate? Not unless you like paying substantially more for a property.

■ *CAUTION NOTE: Unusually low interest rates may mean the fee to the bank is hidden in the selling price.*

In a variation of this arrangement, the bank makes the below-market interest rate good only for a year or two, after which the interest rates go back to their current level. Again, to get this loan either you or the builder will pay a big fee up front. This, too, might be all right . . . if you want a big shock several years down the road.

■ *CAUTION NOTE: Initially low rates may mean higher ones for the long term.*

In the next chapter we will learn about the advantages of adjustable rate mortgages and how to negotiate them with your bank.

WHAT YOU NEED TO KNOW ABOUT ADJUSTABLE RATE LOANS

7

In Chapter 2 we introduced "adjustable" mortgages, officially called adjustable rate mortgages (ARM) or variable rate loans (VRL). They are the newest and most complicated forms of mortgages. In all adjustable mortgages the interest rate is allowed to vary according to an interest rate index. Lenders raise and lower the interest rate on the mortgage based on similar increases and decreases in the index. These mortgage plans usually contain limits, called rate caps, on how far the interest rate can change.

■ *KEY POINT:* *In an ARM, the interest rate varies according to a national or regional index.*

ARMs generally have rate caps on two levels: maximum per period (with definition of the period as six months or one year), and life caps—the maximum the lender can raise rates for the entire life of the contract. Too often a "teaser" or initial low rate is removed soon after the mortgage is signed.

■ *CAUTION NOTE:* *Initial low rate on an ARM often escalates quickly.*

Depending on the lender's particular adjustable mortgage program, the change in the interest rate may result in a change in the monthly payment, the loan term, or the balance of the principal. There are many ways in which to vary these loans, but they are all tied to a national economic index. As this index

113

number changes, your rate, hence payment, changes. For example, if you negotiate an adjustable rate loan with a beginning interest rate of 12% and the interest rate of the particular index to which your loan is tied increases, you might suddenly find yourself making payments based on a 13% interest rate. Some banks offer plans in which the interest rate can change every three or six months but the payment only changes every two years. In this case it's possible that the monthly payment won't be enough to cover all the interest due, thereby causing the unpaid interest to be added to the loan balance. This negative amortization can often occur when monthly payments are not adjusted at the same time as the interest rate.

■ *CAUTION NOTE: Payments that do not keep up with the interest rate in an ARM can cause unpaid interest to be added to the loan balance.*

THE DIFFERENT KINDS OF ADJUSTABLE RATE LOANS

Adjustable Rate Mortgage (ARM).   In a typical adjustable rate mortgage, an initial interest rate is negotiated at the beginning of the loan, then adjusted according to the particular index at fixed intervals during the life of the loan. This index may be an accepted indicator of interest rates, such as the current 90-day Treasury bill rate—the interest the U.S. Treasury pays on its short-term borrowing. In this way your monthly payment periodically changes based on fluctuations in the overall monetary indicators.

■ *KEY POINT: A common ARM index is the 90-day Treasury bill rate.*

Whereas the initial rate you pay on an ARM may be lower than on a fixed rate loan, much of the risk in whether rates will rise or fall is assumed by you. The lender needs less protection against a possible rise in rates. Therefore, banks, to encourage you to choose this loan, lend this money out at a slightly lower rate to start.

■ *CAUTION NOTE: In an ARM, the interest rate may be lower to start, but you assume the risk of a possible rise in rates.*

Graduated Payment Mortgage (GPM). Another kind of adjustable loan is the graduated payment mortgage. This loan provides for smaller payments at the beginning, which rise at fixed amounts over a set number of years, often five to ten years.

■ *KEY POINT: In the graduated payment plan, payments rather than interest rates vary.*

In one GPM plan, the payments increase at 6½% each year for the first six years of the loan. Ultimately, the monthly payments will rise above those of a comparable fixed rate mortgage.

The lower payment in the beginning is excellent for a young professional person starting out in an entry-level job—anyone whose salary may be low now but who expects dramatic increases in a few years.

■ *KEY POINT: A GPM allows you to get a mortgage with minimal beginning payments.*

You may wonder when you start paying off the principal. True, in the first few years when the payment is lower, you may not reduce the principal. You may even accumulate negative amortization and pile up more debt. For example, if your original interest rate is 12¾% but your initial monthly payments are lower than what they would normally be at the 12¾% rate, the difference eats up what principal would have been paid, giving you a small deficit which is added to the loan balance. If you started with a $55,000 loan with the lower payment schedule, you might actually owe $56,000 at the end of the first year.

■ *CAUTION NOTE: Negative amortization, the adding on of unpaid interest, can occur in graduated payment plans.*

This small deficit does not mean this loan program is bad. You have had the advantage of smaller payments; you've been able to invest that money elsewhere in the meantime. It's money you're not paying to the bank when your salary is low. Later, when you can afford it, full payments can be made. The money itself is usually added at the end of the loan and you may not plan to keep the property that long.

The disadvantage of this loan is the gamble that your salary will rise. In a few years your payments will increase to the normal payment, based on the interest rate you negotiated at the beginning. At that time the loan will appear more like a fixed rate, conventional loan. You must then have the income to support these higher payments.

■ *CAUTION NOTE: In a GPM you gamble that your salary will increase to meet the larger payments expected later.*

Graduated Payment Adjustable Rate Mortgage. This mortgage combines the fixed increase of payments of the GPM with an adjustable interest rate. As in the GPM, unpaid interest from the early years is added to the loan balance.

In some graduated payment adjustable rate mortgages, payments rise a fixed amount each year for several years; others set lower payments in the beginning years. In this mortgage, as with many adjustable loans, there are many variations.

■ *KEY POINT: Like the GPM, the graduated payment adjustable rate mortgage sets payment increases and adds unpaid interest to the loan balance.*

Pledged-Account Mortgage (PAM). The pledged-account mortgage is a special kind of graduated payment loan. It is a way in which the unpaid interest, instead of being added onto the loan balance, is automatically withdrawn from a savings account pledged by the borrower. A portion of the borrower's down payment is used to create the savings account.

■ *KEY POINT:* *Pledged account mortgages call for a savings account to be pledged for the unpaid interest.*

Elastic Mortgage. A loan similar to the adjustable rate loan is the flexible or elastic mortgage. In this mortgage the payments are fixed at a set amount in the same way as a fixed rate loan. However, the interest rate upon which these payments are originally based changes according to a chosen government index. Fixed payments but varying rates change the number of payments you make over the life of the mortgage. If the interest rate declines you will need fewer payments to pay off the same balance. For example, an elastic mortgage with a term of 20 years originally set at 13% will be paid off more quickly, perhaps in 18 years, if the rate drops to 11%.

■ *KEY POINT:* *In an elastic mortgage, payments remain the same but the payment term varies.*

In an elastic mortgage you make principal payments more quickly as interest rates drop; if rates increase, you pay off less principal, thereby taking more time for your fixed payments to pay off the loan.

■ *CAUTION NOTE:* *A rising index causes less principal to be paid, thereby adding payments to the loan.*

This plan combines some of the advantages of both the adjustable rate and the fixed conventional rate loans. The payments stay the same, but you can gamble on interest rates fluctuating in the marketplace. The loan is popular with lenders, because, just as in an ARM, it unburdens them of the risk of changing rates. It also begins with a slightly lower interest rate.

Growing Equity Mortgage (GEM).   Another adjustable loan is called the growing equity mortgage. In a GEM, the equity in your house increases at a faster rate than it normally would under either a constant payment or flexible rate loan. You actually pay a little bit more each year, thus reducing the principal.

This increased amount is based on a predetermined percent. For example, 6% each year means your loan gets paid off in considerably less time than the originally scheduled term of the loan. The 25-year term might therefore be reduced to 14 or 15 years.

■ *KEY POINT: The higher payments of a growing equity mortgage reduce the principal faster.*

Shared-Appreciation Mortgage (SAM).   In a shared-appreciation mortgage, a lender, in exchange for a lower rate of interest, shares in the property's increase in value. A variation of this is for the lender to share in the equity of the property.

■ *KEY POINT: In a shared-appreciation mortgage, the lender shares in the property's increase in value in return for giving a low interest rate.*

In return for sharing in the property's appreciation, the lender gives the borrower a lower rate of interest than that on a conventional fixed rate mortgage. SAMs usually require that a portion of the interest due be contingent upon property appreciation. When the property is sold, refinanced, or has matured, the borrower must pay the lender the agreed-upon share of the appreciation. Payments on SAMs are long term but may balloon in five to ten years, depending upon what is negotiated when the loan is set up.

■ *CAUTION NOTE: Depending upon the agreement, a SAM may allow the loan balance to balloon before the end of the term.*

With most banks you can negotiate what the interest rate will be, the term of the mortgage, and how much appreciation they will receive. Since future appreciation is unknown, the difference between the initial interest rate and the effective, or real, rate is difficult to predict. Initially low payments may increase dramatically if the lender's share of appreciation and loan balance are refinanced at a conventional rate.

■ *KEY POINT: Most banks offering SAMs allow you to negotiate interest rate, terms, and amount of appreciation due.*

In choosing a shared-appreciation mortgage, you must weigh the value of the lower interest rate against the potential appreciation you will forfeit. If average fixed rates are 13% and you're only offered a 11½% loan, it's of no benefit to you if you have to give up one-quarter of any appreciation, particularly if neighboring property has been rising 5 and 6% per year. The 1½% interest is a small price to pay to gain all the increase in value for yourself.

There are other variations of the adjustable rate or adjustable payment loan. If you feel any of these are of benefit to you, discuss them fully with your banker. Be aware that the adjustable rate loan often tends to favor the bank. That's why they push it so hard and discount points so easily. They want you to take the risk—the risk of whether rates rise or fall.

■ *CAUTION NOTE: Many adjustable rate or adjustable payment mortgages favor the lender.*

When interest rates are high and you feel they will come down, then consider one of these loans. However, if rates are down and inevitably will rise, the risk may not be worth it. Let's see what precautions you can take to protect yourself in assuming the risk of an ARM.

WHY THEY HAVE SUBSTANTIALLY LOWER RATES

The intitial interest rate on an adjustable or variable rate mortgage, like a fixed rate loan, is based on the lender's cost of funds, specifically on what the bank must pay to its depositors or another bank.

Historically, mortgage interest rates have not risen much except in the last 20 years. The modern, robust economy has put the banks under great inflationary pressure. They need to protect themselves against the rising tide of higher interest rates. Therefore, they have invented "adjustable" loans tied to national indices.

■ *CAUTION NOTE: Adjustable loans are predicated on the theory that rates will continue to rise.*

To induce you to opt for the adjustable rate loan, the banks offer a substantially lower interest rate in the beginning. For a set period of up to a year, it may be two or three points below the rate the bank charges for a fixed rate mortgage. Sometimes it is four or five points below the fixed rate. However, after an initial grace period, any of these lower rates can change dramatically, by 1½ to 2 percentage points a year. Sometimes the cut-rate bonuses of four or five points disappear within a year. To protect yourself, study them and discuss carefully with your banker and lawyer the fine print of any of these adjustable rate mortgages to see exactly how they are structured.

■ *CAUTION NOTE: Lenders offer low initial rates on adjustable loans because they want you to borrow this way.*

■ *CAUTION NOTE: After the first several years, rates on adjustable loans can rise significantly.*

LESS RISK THAN YOU THINK

Much of what's been said so far about adjustable rate mortgages has been derogatory. They have their place, but the problem with them is that many of their early, low rates are simply inducements that soon vanish.

These programs are popular, primarily because they're heavily promoted by the banks. Essentially an adjustable rate loan protects the bank against interest rates rising. And rates have traditionally risen; throughout this century, rates have slowly increased. It's true that rates go down from time to time. You can benefit from short-term fluctuations. So to benefit with an ARM, you've got to hit it when rates are high and hope for a low soon.

■ *CAUTION NOTE: Adjustable loans protect banks from rising interest rates.*

The news, then, is not all bad. A few years ago, rates reached peaks of 17 and 18%. Currently, they are lower, since inflation has eased. They may continue to slide for the short term. If this continues, you may benefit. For example, if you start a loan at 14%, it's conceivable that the index that determines this rate will slowly decrease, bringing your rate down to 12%, thereby lowering your payments or reducing the amount of principal on your loan.

■ *KEY POINT: You can benefit in the short term if you get an ARM when rates are high but about to decrease.*

RATES ARE TIED TO THE MONEY MARKET

The index that determines your rate, albeit indirectly, can vary depending on what it is. A common index is the 90-day Treasury bill rate—what the U.S. Treasury pays on its short-term borrowing. Another indicator is based on long-term treasury loans. Another is the home loan bank board's national average mortgage contract percent. A more stable and less variable rate than some of these is the rate on a 3-year U.S. Treasury security. In some way, each indicator is tied to an overall national market for money. As each varies, the particular rate of your ARM is adjusted at fixed intervals.

■ *KEY POINT: Adjustable mortgages can be tied to one of various national indicators.*

In some ARM agreements, lenders have the right to change the index during the course of a loan. A lender would only do this to gain a higher interest rate for the bank. Check your mortgage agreement closely to see that only one index is used for the life of the loan. You don't want the rules changed midway through the game.

■ *CAUTION NOTE: Some ARM agreements allow the lender to change indices during the loan.*

RATE FLUCTUATION

It's almost impossible to predict at the onset of a loan which way interest rates will go. But people often choose an adjustable rate mortgage because they feel rates will go down. However, one must be prepared for either possibility.

■ *CAUTION NOTE: Rates in the national marketplace can fluctuate significantly.*

As a rough rule, rising inflation causes higher rates, while falling inflation lowers rates. It's hard to come to any fixed rule on this; short-term fluctuations in the national economy are among the many factors which influence mortgage interest.

■ *KEY POINT: Inflation is the biggest factor affecting interest rates.*

The interest amount on the mortgage you negotiate will be with you for a long time. During 30 years, for example, a number of rises and falls will occur in the mortgage market. But rates have historically risen and this trend is likely to continue.

■ *CAUTION NOTE: Over the long term, rates are likely to rise.*

HOW TO PROTECT YOURSELF AGAINST RISING RATES

In an ARM, you must protect yourself as much as possible against rising rates. To do this, you negotiate a provision within the mortgage agreement that controls any skyrocketing of your interest rate. This limits the amount of each adjustment that can be made to your interest rate. For example, your ARM might call for the interest rate to be reviewed quarterly or every six months. A limit on the amount your interest rate can change might be ½ of 1%.

■ *KEY POINT: Negotiate a limit on how much the interest rate can rise during any one period.*

A harsh change would be a movement of 2 or 3%. In most cases you'd like to minimize the limit during an adjustment period and maximize the limit during a period of falling interest rates. Choosing the limit should be based on how you expect rates to behave.

The second limit you want is an overall amount over the life of the loan which your interest rate or monthly payment can be raised. A limit, or cap, of three points over a 25-year period would seem favorable; in contrast, with an upward limit of eight or ten points, or in a mortgage with no cap at all, your loan could get quite expensive.

■ *KEY POINT: Negotiate an overall limit on the rise of the interest rate during the term of the mortgage.*

This limit is normally on the interest rate, but it can also be on the dollar amount you pay each month. Make sure to protect yourself against the unlimited rise of interest rate or payment by having these provisions in your adjustable rate mortgage.

ADVANTAGES AND DISADVANTAGES OF ARMs

The biggest disadvantage of an adjustable rate mortgage is having your interest rate tied to an economic index over which you have no control. Traditionally rates have risen. If your income is relatively low now but will be higher in the future, then it might be reasonable to take advantage of an ARM.

■ *CAUTION NOTE: In an adjustable mortgage, you have no control over the interest rate.*

In an ARM you may be constantly worried about changes in the index that your rate follows and the current mortgage market. The reason bankers promote ARMs is because it takes the gamble out of lending you the money and places the risks of higher payments upon your shoulders.

■ *CAUTION NOTE:* *In an ARM, you assume the risk of higher rates.*

The main advantage of this type of loan is twofold. First, if you are willing to gamble that interest rates are going to go down, you may benefit if the rates decrease. If you are thinking of selling your home within a few years, then the risk of rising rates may not seem so important.

■ *KEY POINT:* *If rates go down, you benefit by having an adjustable loan.*

The second advantage is that the initial interest rate is slightly lower than what is charged for a fixed rate loan. Depending on the amount of this difference, usually 1½ to 2½ points, this can be a real plus in getting started, particularly if this lower rate doesn't automatically end in a set time such as in a year and revert back to a normal rate.

■ *KEY POINT:* *You benefit by a lower initial rate in an adjustable loan.*

Now we'll discuss some ways in which you can negotiate with lenders to make the ARM of more benefit to you. We'll see how to tailor-make an adjustable rate loan that will save you money.

CONVERTING TO A FIXED RATE: THE RENEGOTIABLE MORTGAGE

A fairly recent wrinkle in variable rate plans is called the renegotiable mortgage. Popular several years ago, they are a variation of the adjustable rate mortgage that truly benefits borrowers. Unfortunately, they were too good. Now, they are not widely available but are still offered at some banks.

A renegotiable mortgage has a more conservative schedule than most adjustable mortgages. The amount the interest can change is limited. For example, the rate might swing no more than 1½% every two years and no more than 5% over the entire life of the mortgage. Minimizing the change protects you against unreasonable swings.

■ *KEY POINT:* *Renegotiable mortgages limit the swings in interest rates.*

The rate changing at less frequent intervals than the adjustable rate mortgage and then only adjusting every two to five years can be a great advantage during those periods when interest rates are rising.

A variation of the renegotiable rate mortgage allows the rate itself to be negotiated at specific intervals during the life of the mortgage. For example, you might receive notification from your bank every three years—at this time, the prime interest rate can be converted to the prevailing fixed rate of interest. Your current rate might be 12% and fixed rate loans might be 10%, thereby giving you the option to reduce your rate.

■ *KEY POINT:* *Some renegotiable mortgages allow the interest rate to be negotiated at certain intervals.*

You could also choose to convert to the fixed rate, which conceivably could be the same.

■ *KEY POINT:* *Renegotiable mortgages allow the option of converting to a fixed rate.*

Most renegotiable rate mortgages lock in the rate for several years. In this way they are more conservative than the full adjustable rate mortgages. They combine the benefits of an adjustable rate and a fixed rate loan. With them, you can take advantage of a downward slide in interest rates and also have some security of rising interest rates.

■ *KEY POINT: Renegotiable mortgages combine the best of adjustable and fixed rate loans.*

The renegotiable rate mortgage with an optional conversion to fixed rate may be the loan program for you if you think that the burden of fluctuating payments may prove too much of a struggle some years into the mortgage.

THE ADJUSTABLE BALLOON MORTGAGE

Another variation of the adjustable mortgage is the balloon mortgage. It is similar to a fixed rate loan in that it starts with a set interest rate and a term of 25 or 30 years. However, at the end of a specific period of time, perhaps five years, the mortgage "balloons." This means the loan must be paid off, or, as is commonly done, the amount is refinanced at the current interest rate—in this way it is an adjustable loan.

■ *KEY POINT: Balloon mortgages call for a new interest rate to be negotiated when the loan "balloons."*

In only a few years not much principal will have been paid. In fact, you will owe an amount close to the original loan that must now be paid to the lender. Banks like to use this technique, particularly if they are nervous about what's happening to the cost of money and their ability to get it. In this case you may have no choice. Sometimes it may be the only type of loan you can negotiate.

What happens when the money is due? In most balloon mortgages, particularly with banks, the entire loan—interest rate, terms, everything—is renegotiated. It does, however, put you at the mercy of the current rate being charged at the time of renegotiation.

From a bank's point of view, a balloon mortgage is more flexible than a renegotiable mortgage. Here there aren't any limits on what the interest will be. As a borrower of a balloon mortgage, you take the gamble that rates won't skyrocket. Without a strict provision in the mortgage agreement, the bank can demand some or all of the money. This forces you to come up with cash or go to another bank to borrow the difference.

■ *CAUTION NOTE:* *Make sure the mortgage agreement allows the loan to be refinanced at the "balloon" time.*

Normally, you can refinance the balance and, again, these terms should be spelled out specifically in the mortgage agreement. Sometimes you can negotiate a lower interest rate because of the low ratio of the amount you borrow at the time of renegotiation compared with the higher value of the property. If, when you renegotiate, the value of your property has risen and you only need to borrow 50 or 60%, you give the bank excellent security, thereby enhancing your chance not only for the continuation of the loan but also for a lower rate.

■ *KEY POINT:* *An advantage at renegotiation time is that the property's value will likely have risen.*

As in the renegotiable rate loan, you want a guarantee that you can refinance it and, if possible, a limit on how much the interest rate can change.

NEGOTIATING MANAGEABLE PAYMENTS

The reason for having an adjustable rate loan is to beat the current long-term rate. However, adjustable loans were created by banks to do just the opposite. The banks intend to use these instruments to protect themselves; be aware that they want you to assume the risk.

Unfortunately, at some banks they are the only type of loan available at a reasonable price, the fixed rate loan having been made prohibitively expensive. These banks charge much more for interest in a fixed rate loan than they do in an ARM; they also pile up points on the fixed rate loan. You are not offered much of a choice—they want you to take the ARM.

■ *CAUTION NOTE:* *By charging more interest for fixed rate loans banks force you to choose an adjustable mortgage.*

It's therefore essential for you to know the ins and outs of how to negotiate an adjustable loan. The information here will prepare you.

If an ARM's adjustment period—when the interest rate is reviewed—is every quarter or six months, ask to have that period extended to a year. Then you can plan more, perhaps refinancing, renegotiating a longer term, or switching to a conventional loan if the rate swings the wrong way. In any event, the full year gives you a longer period in which to plan.

■ *KEY POINT:* *Longer adjustment periods tend to benefit the borrower.*

Be aware, in any ARM, that the rate generally moves down more slowly than it moves up. Just as an excess of oil may take some time to drive the price of petroleum down in world markets, it may take a good while before the benefits of lower rates are passed on to you. However, if the cost of oil rises, it usually doesn't take too long before there are higher prices at the gasoline pump. The same sort of double standard is at work with interest rates. Banks are rarely enthusiastic about lowering rates. Most are profit-making organizations and will jump at the chance to increase their rates faster than they will to reduce them. However, you know the index that determines your rate, and with a little perseverance you can make sure they drop it as fast as they increase it.

■ *CAUTION NOTE:* **Banks are faster to raise interest rates than lower them.**

HOW TO PROTECT YOURSELF AGAINST THE PITFALLS OF ARMs

One of the first pitfalls of an adjustable rate mortgage is that the interest rate is intricately tied to a particular index. Whatever this index is, it affects your monthly payment. The best protection is to ensure, via negotiation, that your rate is limited to reasonable jumps for periods that are as long as possible. For example, a reasonable limit might be one and a half percentage points over four or five years, with a total increase limit of 5 or 6% over the life of the loan. In this way you are assured that the increase isn't open-ended.

■ *KEY POINT:* **Limit interest rate movements to reasonable swings.**

In ten years, you don't want to end up paying twice as much because your interest rate is adjustable. You protect yourself by negotiating reasonable limits.

As we've seen, in some variable rate plans, such as the graduated payment mortgage, negative amortization can occur—you might not be paying enough to meet your interest obligation and therefore the difference will be added on to the balance of the loan. In the beginning, your payments are set artificially low. Although this may seem like a bonus for the first few years, the interest you're not paying is added to your loan balance, so you can end up paying more than your starting loan balance. However, if your income will rise to meet the later payments, negative amortization can be turned into an advantage.

■ *KEY POINT: Negative amortization can be a plus or a minus, depending on how much income you will make in the future.*

Another advantage of ARMs is that banks minimize origination points or prepayment penalties. Since you're shouldering the risk, they don't want to add more burden. They want you to opt for the adjustable plan so badly they don't want to make it seem expensive.

■ *KEY POINT: Few or no origination points or prepayment penalties are paid with an adjustable mortgage.*

If prepayment points are included, fight to eliminate them. At the very least try to negotiate a guarantee that they not be charged later, for example, upon refinancing or sale of the property.

It's possible you might want a new buyer to assume your loan in the future. Transferring an ARM is easier to negotiate with the bank, since the rate is already tied to the chosen index. Try to have this provision spelled out in the mortgage agreement.

■ *KEY POINT: No prepayment penalty makes it easier to negotiate for your loan to be taken over by a new buyer in the future.*

Banks seem willing to do most anything to get you to borrow their money on an adjustable basis. After all, they don't usually require the points charged in their conventional fixed rate loan. This makes the ARM look too good to be true. If anything, this tips you off that the banks will somehow benefit—there's a cost to everything. And in an ARM it's the hidden cost you must protect yourself against.

■ *CAUTION NOTE:* **In an adjustable mortgage you must protect yourself against the hidden cost of a rising interest rate.**

In the next chapter, we will explore creative financing by sellers.

WHEN THE SELLER GIVES YOU THE MORTGAGE

8

The most readily available mortgage money is already in the property. This equity is owned by the seller. Your mortgage may be there for the asking.

HELP FROM THE SELLER: A TWO-WAY ADVANTAGE

The seller is in the best position to loan you money and should always be asked to do so.

Often real estate agents say sellers aren't interested in giving mortgages. This frequently just isn't true. In times when money is tight, interest rates are high, and the banks are making few loans, if any at all, sellers must help out with the financing. Just to make a sale they must often give either a full first mortgage or help with secondary financing, whether it involves a residential home, an investment property, a vacation home, or even a lot. Many are ready to make mortgage deals.

■ *KEY POINT: Sellers are willing to give some form of financing more often than not.*

What are some of the many ways sellers can help you finance? The most popular is the second mortgage, where you

133

borrow the difference between what a bank lends and how much you invest as a down payment. For example, the second mortgage may only be 10–15% of the purchase price, for a relatively short term of five or ten years, and set at an interest rate near the rate for the first mortgage.

■ *KEY POINT:* *Second mortgages are the most common form of seller financing.*

Another common variation of the second mortgage bases the monthly payment on a long-term payoff, such as over 20 or 30 years. However, the balance comes due in a shorter time, perhaps in three to five years. This ballooning usually works because the amount of the second mortgage is relatively small compared with the first mortgage. You can come up with this balloon payment either by refinancing with the bank that holds the first mortgage or borrowing on a short-term basis from a commercial bank. Either way, equity has built up in your property, more than enough to secure any increase in mortgage funds.

■ *KEY POINT:* *Second mortgages are often accompanied by balloon-payment provisions.*

■ *CAUTION NOTE:* *Prepare ahead of time to meet the balloon payment.*

Buyers and sellers can work out financing in numerous ways. One popular arrangement is for the seller to take back a fixed rate first mortgage, also called a purchase money mortgage. This works well when the seller doesn't have any more than a small mortgage on the property. He or she can change this equity into a mortgage. This often happens in business property, such as in a small apartment building where the owner is ready to retire and still willing to continue a steady return on investment. He or she can do this by giving you the mortgage. The seller changes the investment he has from a physical asset to one on paper—a mortgage guaranteeing a steady income at a good interest rate.

■ *KEY POINT:*   *Seller financing benefits both buyer and seller.*

You can also take over a seller's existing financing. You assume or take the mortgage "subject to." Before you approach the bank on any specific takeover, go over every detail of the present mortgage agreement with the seller.

■ *KEY POINT:*   *Assuming a seller's existing mortgage often gets you a low interest rate.*

Normally any proposed purchase is conditional upon your getting conventional financing from a bank or the seller. If the seller is anxious to make the sale, he is more likely to allow you to assume his loan or give you some amount of the sale price as a second mortgage, sometimes even giving you a full first mortgage. Whether you buy direct or use a real estate agent, always try the seller first.

■ *KEY POINT:*   *Always ask the seller about financing.*

ASSUMING THE SELLER'S MORTGAGE

As we saw in Chapter 3, you as a buyer can take the seller's place. You can assume or take "subject to" the financing the seller negotiated at the time he or she originally bought the property. Your main reason to take over is to get a lower interest rate and more favorable terms than those you could presently negotiate.

■ *KEY POINT:*   *Assume the seller's loan when you can.*

Assuming a loan means you accept all legal obligations from the seller. Taking the existing loan "subject to" means the seller's name remains on the loan and you're simply making payments for him, thereby accepting less legal liability yourself.

■ *KEY POINT: Officially, "assuming" means accepting legal responsibility; "subject to" means sharing liability.*

Does transferring a loan hurt the seller? Not at all. He can get his property sold and you as a buyer get both the loan and a favorable interest rate.

In assuming a loan you often must put up more cash than you would if you took out a new mortgage. You have to weigh a larger down payment but lower payments of the existing loan against a smaller down payment but higher payments due to a bigger loan and higher interest rate on a new loan. For example, if you take out a new, 20-year, fixed rate mortgage for $60,000 at 13%, your monthly payments would be $702.95, instead of $564.09 for the same balance on an older 8% loan. Furthermore, in assuming an existing loan, the balance will be paid off faster and equity will accordingly build more quickly. Granted, you can often borrow more than the old balance on a new loan, but there is a big difference in payments due to the higher interest rate.

■ *CAUTION NOTE: Assuming an existing loan may mean a larger down payment.*

■ *KEY POINT: The advantages include lower monthly payments, faster equity buildup, and less time until maturity.*

To take advantage of the lower rate but not have such a large down payment, negotiate a second mortgage in addition to the takeover. You can do this with the seller or the bank.

■ *KEY POINT: A second mortgage can make up the difference between the loan you assume and a reasonable down payment.*

In any second mortgage, you may likely pay more in interest than on a new first mortgage. This is because a second mortgage holder's claim on the property comes after the claim secured by the first mortgage. You may pay a higher rate for your $5,000, $10,000, or even $20,000 mortgage. However, you get a substantially lower rate on the first mortgage. You are still better off than if you got a single first mortgage for the full amount at current mortgage rates.

■ *CAUTION NOTE: Sometimes sellers want more interest on a second mortgage when they allow you to assume the existing, first mortgage.*

You're not always permitted to assume a conventional mortgage loan. In the late 1960s and early 1970s, banks got wise to take-overs and assumptions and began putting in their mortgage agreements clauses to prevent a new buyer from taking over existing financing. However, many older mortgages can still be assumed. Even newer loans, due to their higher rates, can be taken over with the bank's permission.

■ *CAUTION NOTE: Banks often have clauses preventing take-overs in their mortgage agreements.*

■ *KEY POINT: Many older loans can still be taken over.*

THE TRADITIONAL SECOND MORTGAGE

We've already talked about second mortgages in connection with other loans. They are often what makes other loans work. For most buyers, the second mortgage helps make up the difference between the down payment and the first mortgage.

■ *KEY POINT: A second mortgage is often what makes seller financing work.*

The first mortgage is first in the line of security in case of default and subsequent foreclosure on the loan. The payback on a first mortgage is made before the second, third, or other mortgages. The second mortgage, since it is subordinate to the first, often has a slightly higher interest rate due to this extra risk. No set rule applies; often, if the seller is anxious to sell the rate might be slightly less than current rates.

■ *CAUTION NOTE:* *The higher rate of a second mortgage is commensurate with the extra risk involved.*

Sometimes a considerable down payment must be made upon assuming a loan. The existing loan might be only 30 or 40% of the selling price. You might only have 10 or 20% to put down as a down payment. The difference should be negotiated as a second mortgage with the seller.

■ *KEY POINT:* *Assuming a second mortgage often requires a larger down payment.*

In most cases the seller is willing to give the second mortgage on an assumption. This depends greatly on her motivation. If the seller doesn't need the cash to purchase another house, she can benefit from the interest, particularly if the rate is more than she could get in bonds or certificates of deposit. After all, the seller shouldn't be worried about the value of her second mortgage, since it's secured by the property itself. And she sets the selling price. If anyone believes in the property's value, hence the second mortgage, it should be the seller.

■ *KEY POINT:* *A reasonable interest rate on a second mortgage is usually more than the seller can get elsewhere.*

Beyond asking the seller to take the first mortgage, the second mortgage is a likely alternative for the seller to agree to. For example, when your new 80% bank loan isn't quite enough because you only have 15% to put down, it's not uncommon for the seller to help you with that extra 5%. If the property sells for $150,000, the $7,500 the seller loans you, let's say over five years with quarterly payments at an interest rate no more than the bank is charging, can be a real help in getting the right property.

■ *KEY POINT:* *Rates for second mortgages given by sellers are usually equal to or a point above the bank's rate.*

As we've seen, a seller will often want a second mortgage to balloon after a few years so he or she can get the money out. The seller doesn't usually want to lend the money for as long as a bank. But to keep payments lower, long-term plans in which the balance comes due in a shorter period are negotiated.

■ *KEY POINT:* *The ballooning of the balance must be prepared for but keeps you from being overwhelmed with large payments.*

There's no difference between buying an investment or commercial property with a second mortgage and buying a house. In fact, the businessperson is likely to be more familiar with holding a mortgage, thereby willing to give a larger amount than a homeowner.

The owner of a business property may live in the same community. He or she may feel more secure in holding the mortgage on a property that can be seen and inspected.

■ *KEY POINT:* *Owners of investment property often feel more secure in giving a second mortgage.*

A builder's new house or condominium can often be bought with secondary financing. The builder may already have arranged for attractive bank financing at below-market rates and as further encouragement makes up a 5–10% difference in a second mortgage.

■ *KEY POINT:* *Builders often plan on helping buyers of new homes by giving second mortgages.*

Again, in negotiating any mortgage, particularly with a private party, make sure that you have a competent attorney to do the necessary legal work, such as a title search to make sure there are no other encumbrances upon the property you are buying. You also want your lawyer to make sure that any written agreement is specific and clearly understandable. The lawyer will also see to it that the mortgage is recorded in the local registry of deeds.

■ *CAUTION NOTE:* *Always consult with an attorney when arranging secondary financing.*

Any time you buy with financing provided by the seller, the provisions are included as part of the purchase offer. So, when the offer is accepted, the financing is too. This provision need be nothing more than a sentence within the offer form. In most legal jurisdictions, formal papers detailing the actual terms of the mortgage agreement are drawn up by the lawyers ten days to two weeks after the offer form has been signed by both parties. In this more formal purchase and sale agreement, the financing provision may be spelled out in more detail but must reflect the provision contained in the offer form.

■ *KEY POINT:* *Seller financing is negotiated at the same time as purchase price and terms.*

Second mortgages are the most frequent form of financing help given by a seller to a buyer in the United States. Estimates are that over half of all residential and business sales includes secondary financing.

THE WRAPAROUND MORTGAGE AND HOW IT WORKS

Wraparound or all-inclusive mortgages are mortgages taken back by the seller or institutional lender with the existing financing. They are a form of second mortgage; a first mortgage is already on the property and the wraparound is in a secondary position. It is sometimes called an overriding trustee or overriding mortgage.

■ *KEY POINT: Wraparound mortgages include existing and new financing.*

How does a wraparound mortgage work? Here's one scenario. The seller of a small apartment building has an existing loan with a balance of $40,000 at 8½% and 20 years left to pay. He agrees to sell it to you for $80,000, with you putting up $15,000 in cash. This leaves $25,000 to be financed. You could refinance the first mortgage of $40,000 to a higher amount. However, you likely would pay a much higher interest rate, but perhaps money is tight and the bank isn't willing to extend itself beyond the existing $40,000. One possibility is to assume the existing loan of $40,000 and have the seller carry back a second mortgage for the remaining $25,000.

A better alternative is to construct a wraparound mortgage. For example, the seller agrees to a mortgage of $65,000 at a rate between the old rate of 8½% and the current rate of 14% charged by the banks—10%, for instance. In the written agreement detailing the provisions, a clause will state this mortgage includes the unpaid balance of the existing first mortgage and that the seller is still responsible for making these payments. He must make payments on the existing $40,000 at the 8½% out of the payment he receives from you on the $65,000 mortgage at 10%.

■ *KEY POINT: In a wraparound mortgage, the seller is often still responsible for paying the existing loan.*

The advantage to the seller is the percentage point and a half he makes as profit, plus a full 10% on the $25,000 difference. As the buyer, you benefit too. Although you don't get the 8½% on the existing $40,000—it is 10% overall—you've saved quite a bit, considering the current market rate. You have also avoided any prepayment penalties that might have been charged by an institutional lender.

■ *KEY POINT: Wraparounds save interest and points.*

The wraparound can also be an excellent technique when the existing mortgage has a low interest rate and is assumable. Let's say an $85,000 property has a 10-year-old first mortgage with a balance of $40,000 at 8% interest. You, the buyer, are willing to put down a $15,000 deposit. That leaves a balance of $30,000. Instead of the seller giving you a straight second mortgage for this $30,000, as he might be willing to if the first $40,000 could be assumed, the seller gives a wraparound, an overall mortgage which includes the first mortgage and a hypothetical (the amount of the normal second) second totaling $70,000.

The incentive for you is that the overall interest rate for the wraparound is less than current bank rates. If the current rate is 14% and you and the seller settle on an overall interest rate of 11%, the seller benefits because he's making three points of interest over the old loan. This is better for him than if you assumed his loan and got a new mortgage of $40,000 and if he then had to give you a second mortgage for the remaining $30,000, even though the second mortgage might carry an interest rate closer to the current rate.

■ *KEY POINT: Wraparounds can also be used to circumvent nonassumable loans.*

The seller, then, is better off by negotiating a wraparound mortgage, even if he receives less than current rates. You benefit because you can't take over the existing mortgage but are able to get the mortgage money you need at favorable rates.

■ *KEY POINT: Both buyer and seller can benefit by negotiating a wraparound.*

The major difficulty with a wraparound or all-inclusive mortgage lies in its limitation to mortgage agreements that lack a "due and payable" clause against the property; the clause may cause trouble if the mortgage is taken over by someone else. Solution: hold the deed in escrow until the loan is paid off. Also, it's always possible the bank might waive this clause and allow the loan to stand.

■ *CAUTION NOTE: It is difficult to "wraparound" all non-assumable loans.*

Wraparounds work when it is difficult to negotiate the price of the property with the seller, but when the seller will allow you to take over the existing financing, which may have a low rate.

WHEN YOU WANT A BOND FOR DEED

A bond for deed, similar to the contract for deed discussed in Chapter 3, is another way to get around an institutional lender's non-assumable "due on sale" clause in a mortgage agreement. In a bond for deed sale, the property is held in escrow by a title company or lawyer. It is not recorded, since this would trigger the non-assumable clause within the mortgage. You as the buyer make payments to the previous owner. He, in turn, gives these payments to the bank; it is under his name that the mortgage is held. A down payment or second mortgage is given to the seller.

■ *KEY POINT:*   *A bond for deed transaction involves seller financing with the deed held in escrow.*

■ *KEY POINT:*   *A bond for deed gets around non-assumable loan clauses.*

As with many existing mortgages, there may be less than a 50% balance left and an excellent interest rate that is desirable to take over. The disadvantage, however minor, is that the title is not in your name. Therefore, you must have legal assurances from the seller that the money you give him will be used to pay off the loan.

■ *CAUTION NOTE:*   *Gain assurance from seller that your payments to him will go to pay the existing mortgage.*

As with any sale where the seller gives the financing, the bond for deed is negotiated on the same offer form as the selling price. You get an instantaneous loan acceptance without the need for a separate financial proposal.

■ *KEY POINT:*   *A bond for deed sale involves instant financing.*

WHEN A LEASE WITH OPTION MAKES SENSE

Another way to take over an existing loan is to lease the property with an option to take over formal ownership in the future. You pay all expenses, including the mortgage, while gaining full use of the property. A favored technique for many buyers of investment property, it can also work in taking over a private residence.

■ *KEY POINT: A lease with option gives control while deferring the actual sale.*

Technically, you only lease the property, but when you have an option to buy you have much more authority and control than the average tenant. It is a way to take over a property with no money down. You don't have to give the seller any down payment, although you may give money for the option. You pay a negotiated monthly rent. If it's an income property, this fee will be based on how much money is left over after you have collected the tenant's rent and paid all operating expenses, including the mortgage.

■ *CAUTION NOTE: You may pay the seller money for option rights.*

All the operating costs, including the bank payments, will in most cases be directly made by you; this ensures that they are being made and also establishes your control.

The option to purchase often cites a time by which you must buy; it might also be open-ended. You might not have to assume ownership until you wish to transfer the property to another buyer, or, if you wish, you may not purchase at all.

■ *KEY POINT: Sometimes the time to take up the option is not established, allowing you to sell to another buyer.*

It's the easiest way to take over a mortgage. Even if the loan is non-assumable, the lender cannot call it, since the original owner still officially has the title. You are simply leasing the property and making payments directly to the bank on behalf of the holder of the title. If you and the seller agree, the deed could be signed over to you and held in escrow.

■ *KEY POINT: A lease with option is an easy way to take over the responsibility of a non-assumable mortgage.*

Often the purpose of the lease with option arrangement is to approximate a sale with the attributes of a transfer without the actual transfer of the deed. It could also be done to give you a period of time to become familiar with the operation of the buildings. If it's an income property, you might want some time to study its management, handling the operation and relations with tenants before taking full title to the property.

■ *KEY POINT: A lease with option gives you time to become familiar with the property.*

Here's how a lease with option might work. You agree to lease with an option of $200,000 an eight-unit apartment building. The existing loan, at a favorable 7½%, has been paid down to $110,000. It was originally for 20 years, and since the present owners have owned the property for 10 years, the loan has 10 more years to go. If you had to refinance this $110,000 (even though you could probably get more money than that, ie, up to $150,000), you would have to pay 15% or more in interest.

You negotiate with the seller a rent that approximates the amount paid if you had a second mortgage with him. If you give him a $10,000 "down payment" as a sign that you will perform on your option, that leaves a difference from the $110,000 first mortgage of $80,000. If this $80,000 were invested at current rates of 14% for 10 years, you would earn $14,905.58 annually, $1,242.13 monthly. This amount, then, is the rent you pay the seller under the terms of your lease. It is constructed as a second mortgage so that should you take over the property prior to the end of the 10 years, the balance would become due.

This arrangement allows you to take over the property and not take title until a future time. The $10,000 down payment could be handled as a security deposit, an amount guaranteeing that you will follow through with the terms of the lease. In many areas, when a lease runs more than five or ten years, it must be recorded in the local county Registry of Deeds as a formal document.

■ *KEY POINT: Long-term leases are often recorded in the local Registry of Deeds.*

Another way the lease with option could work is to send all monies due on mortgages to the seller, who will make his own payments directly. Or, upon negotiation with him, you may make those payments directly to the bank, thus assuring yourself that they are being made.

■ *KEY POINT: Payment on existing mortgages can be made by you through the seller or directly.*

The disadvantage in leasing is that you are not the owner of record and may not be able to get depreciation deductions that accrue with the ownership of investment property (more on this in Chapter 10). However, IRS regulations imply that long-term leasing is like ownership; if so stipulated in your agreement with the seller, you may be eligible for these deductions. Check with your accountant.

■ *CAUTION NOTE: Leasing does not normally qualify you for depreciation deductions.*

Whether you're a tenant or an owner of an income property, all costs (eg, property taxes, utility charges, snow removal) are deductible as ordinary expenses. The mortgage payments you make are the seller's but are deductible for you if based upon rent that must be paid to him.

■ *KEY POINT: Under most circumstances, business deductions can only be taken by the person paying the bills.*

The lease with option is an excellent technique in taking over a property—the bank is not involved, the investment is minimal, the closing is deferred, and most of the benefits of ownership can be enjoyed in the meantime.

A VARIATION: MANAGEMENT AGREEMENT WITH OPTION (MAO)

Here's another way to take over a property and defer formal financing until later. Like leasing with an option, it's another way for you to get control of a property with no down payment and no financial negotiations with the bank or seller.

The management agreement with option is a technique used to take over larger investment properties that require management expertise. It's not a technique normally used to take over a house; most sellers require cash or a firm commitment on a first or second mortgage before they sell. But it might be used if the seller is willing, particularly if he or she is an absentee businessperson.

■ *CAUTION NOTE: A management agreement with option is not normally used to take over single-family houses.*

In the management agreement with option, you take over the property immediately by virtue of an agreement with the seller to manage the property. In it you assume full control, and continue to do so until you take title; the timetable is specified in your option.

■ *KEY POINT: A management agreement with option gives you full control over the property and tenants.*

Included in the management agreement and option are guarantees ensuring that ultimately the property will be yours. All you need to do is be able to finance it at some agreed-upon time. First, the option to take over the property at a set time in the future is guaranteed. Second, the deed must be signed over to you but held unrecorded in your lawyer's office. Third, you must give some guarantee of performance to the seller, such as a down payment or promissory note. The purchase price is based on the current market.

■ *KEY POINT: MAOS are composed of an option, escrowed deed, and promissory guarantee.*

Fourth, since you may invest money in the property, you want to protect yourself in case of the seller's bankruptcy, since he is the one who technically owns the property. To do this, you negotiate a second mortgage from him to you to cover your down payment (if any) and any additional amount of future equity that will protect your effort. This second mortgage only takes effect in the event of and at the time of the seller's foreclosure (such as a sheriff's sale). This mortgage is recorded. The idea is to protect you from a worst-case scenario. It may seem unlikely but is essential in case of litigation.

■ *KEY POINT: A second mortgage, from the seller to you, effective only in case of the seller's foreclosure, protects your equity and effort.*

Should the worst happen to the seller, endangering the property you now control, your recorded second mortgage takes precedence over other debts. In addition, you may choose to record the deed and take formal possession, depending on your lawyer's advice.

Why bother with an MAO? The answer is an obvious one. How else can you take over a substantial property with little or no down payment? Furthermore, mortgage money may be tight or interest rates high, making it otherwise difficult for you to purchase.

■ *KEY POINT: Like the lease with option, the MAO gives you control.*

A management agreement with option works best on an investment property (apartments or commercial buildings) when institutional money has dried up. You're essentially taking over the property and deferring the negotiation of formal financing until such time as money is more available and rates are better.

■ *KEY POINT: An MAO defers financing until mortgage money is more available and rates are lower.*

In addition, in several years the equity of your property will increase so much that when you go to the bank to get financing, you won't have to put up any additional funds. The future but cheaper money principle makes it easy to pay off the seller.

■ *KEY POINT: Larger equity and cheaper dollars in the future make the past selling price easier to pay.*

You may ask where the seller gets his money from. Until the actual closing, you will be making payments to him based on the criteria you have negotiated in the management agreement. You may negotiate a second mortgage that he holds so that you pay him. What the seller gets is funds that are over and above operating expenses and mortgage payments. You might negotiate to give him what funds are left after you have paid his mortgages and taken a management fee for yourself.

■ *KEY POINT: In an MAO, a second mortgage may be used as an option or down payment.*

This may seem complicated, but it is not. Once explained to the seller, he or she can be very amenable—particularly if motivated to sell but having difficulty in a climate of tight money and high rates.

■ *KEY POINT: An MAO works best for a highly motivated seller of investment or commercial property.*

As you can see, this is an excellent way to take over a property where an existing mortgage cannot be renegotiated favorably or is one that cannot be assumed. It is, in effect, a way to bypass a non-assumable mortgage.

EXCHANGING PROPERTY

Exchanging property is similar to the barter system of ancient days. It usually involves investment property. Two owners can trade their investments, and if those investments are equal in value—what is known as a "like-kind" exchange—under a special provision of the IRS Code, the owners can avoid paying tax on the gain of the sale/exchange at the time of transfer.

■ *KEY POINT: Investors can defer tax when exchanging "like-kind" property.*

Avoiding taxes is not the only reason professional investors exchange property. Another is to keep trading up, getting a larger and larger property. The previous property is used as equity for the newer, larger one. All this can be done without having to sell the first, or exchanged-in, property and triggering taxes.

■ *KEY POINT: Exchanging property is an ideal way to trade up to a larger investment.*

When trading up, the difference in value is usually compensated for by the assumption of an existing and larger mortgage, perhaps a new first mortgage combined with a second mortgage. In some cases, even cash may be used to even the deal.

■ *KEY POINT: In an exchange, only minimal cash may be needed to take over a larger property.*

This technique is thought by many to be a clear path to making a fortune in real estate. The exchange minimizes tax consequences and often the need for additional large down payments. Some investors trade properties several times in a five-year span. Others may do it once in ten years. No matter how often one trades, it is an ideal way to pyramid equity.

■ *KEY POINT: Exchanging "like-kind" property builds rapid equity and defers taxes.*

Note that there is no tax consequence upon the sale of one home and the purchase of another in like-kind exchanges. In most other cases, the owner defers tax on the first residence if this new property (it must be of the same or higher value than the one before) is bought within two years of the sale. This is a special provision in the tax law for residential homes only.

■ *KEY POINT: In trading up homes, taxes can be deferred if the transfer takes place within two years.*

■ *CAUTION NOTE: To defer taxes in an exchange of investment property, the transfer must be at the same time.*

The reason the exchange technique must be used for investment property is that no deferral is allowed upon an actual sale, even though something of equal value and utility is bought. So the IRS allows a tax deferment when a "like-kind" exchange occurs.

■ *CAUTION NOTE: When a non-exchange or straight sale occurs, tax on the gain must be paid during the year of sale.*

Only through the exchange of property, which should always be done in conjunction with a knowledgeable attorney, can you defer taxable gain until such time as you sell the last property you exchanged. It may be years later, when you sell the seventh or eighth exchanged property, before you finally have to pay the tax. But with the diminishing value of the dollar, it still is better for you to pay later.

■ *CAUTION NOTE: Exchanges should only be attempted in conjunction with knowledgeable professionals.*

■ *KEY POINT: Many properties can be exchanged during an extended span of ownership.*

THE EASY WAY TO SELL YOURSELF TO THE SELLER

To get financing from the seller, begin by understanding what his or her motivations are. The fact is that they have the property and you wish to buy it. Now you need to know why it is for sale. Do they simply want to buy something else if the right property comes along? Or must they move because of a job change? Or is the small apartment building you're looking at owned by someone who wants to buy a larger investment? Or has the seller owned the property for a number of years and lost his or her depreciation advantage? Or are financial obligations, like sending children to college or paying doctors' bills, the reason?

The seller who must move or raise cash quickly is highly motivated. You will therefore have an easier time negotiating.

■ *KEY POINT: The seller's motivation is the key to negotiating financing.*

What are some of the other motivations of sellers? The seller may have an expanding family and need a larger house with more bedrooms. Often a divorce will necessitate a property being sold. A commercial or investment building may need repairs that are beyond the capability and funds of the present owner. These are just some of the reasons why owners want to sell. The stronger the motivation of the seller, the easier you can negotiate favorable terms with the seller—to take back financing or otherwise tailor your purchase.

■ *KEY POINT: The stronger the seller's motivation, the more financing help you can get.*

If the seller is not sufficiently motivated, you may not be able to obtain financing this way.

■ *CAUTION NOTE: Without strong motivation, the seller may not be willing to finance.*

HOW TO AVOID THE GAMBLE IN SELLER FINANCING

The key to real estate success, whether the vehicle is a home, investment, parcel of land, or a second home, is financing. Some of the best opportunities are the financing we can get from the sellers. Once you know the seller's motivation, you can construct the best financial terms for you and the seller. Which brings up the following point: There's no reason to do business with the seller unless you can get much better rate and terms than you can from a bank.

■ *KEY POINT: Finance with the seller for a better deal.*

Buyers often look at a selling price and feel if they don't get a bank to approve its value and finance it they've overpaid. This is a fallacy. A bank never validates the selling price of a property for you.

■ *CAUTION NOTE: Don't look to a bank for expert advice on property value.*

The bank is not likely to grant the loan if you overpay, but banks are not value experts—they often base their loan on your ability to make payments and other intangible factors such as whether the market is expanding and whether they'll make a profit. When they're anxious to loan money, they don't look closely at value.

■ *CAUTION NOTE: Banks often overlook property value in granting a loan if they can profit on your payments.*

If they feel you can meet payments and they will profit with interest rates and points, they're likely to extend the loan. That's not any protection against paying too much.

How then do you know you aren't paying more than you should? The answer is twofold. First, in buying any property, you should look at a number of comparable properties in the neighboring area. With a real estate agent squiring you to different houses, you will get a sense of what properties are worth by comparing such qualities as neighborhood, size, and construction.

■ *KEY POINT: Assure yourself of value by comparison shopping.*

Values for houses of similar style and type in the same area don't vary much. At most, they fluctuate a few thousand dollars, and that probably based on extras such as swimming pools and garages.

■ *KEY POINT: The values of similar properties in similar neighborhoods won't vary much.*

The value of an income property is as much on the income it produces after expenses as on its bricks and mortar.

■ *KEY POINT: Much of the value of investment property is based on net income after expenses.*

The second and more important aspect about paying too much is the financing itself. In part, the value of real estate is based on the cost of mortgage financing. Specifically, if interest rates are high, they tend to depress prices; conversely, if rates are low, they inflate prices slightly.

■ *KEY POINT: Contrary to popular opinion, the value of real estate is predicated on the availability of financing.*

■ *CAUTION NOTE: When money is tight and rates are high, property values become depressed.*

Institutional lenders tend to set the "market," that is, the particular interest rate being charged has a direct effect on prices.

What does this mean to you? It means that if you negotiate two or three percentage points off the going bank rate in a mortgage with a seller, your net cost for the deal is less than someone who got a bank mortgage.

■ *KEY POINT: Any time you negotiate a lower-than-normal interest rate, you lower the overall cost of the property.*

This doesn't mean you should pay more for the property in order to get a financing deal with a seller, but it does give you a margin of protection. If a seller provides you a loan at 10% interest when the going rate is 14%, you are benefiting by 4% a year.

This can add up to a substantial savings, which is a big reason for you to attempt to get seller financing. Some investors don't even consider a property if the seller won't offer a substantial amount of financing. It's not that they don't want to do business with a bank; they just want a better rate for their loan and to avoid origination points and prepayment penalties.

■ *KEY POINT: Some investment strategies call for financing through sellers only.*

The key to taking the gamble out of seller financing lies in the motivation of the seller. The higher that motivation, the better deal you will negotiate. Any margin of savings over current interest rates makes your investment cost that much less.

■ *KEY POINT: Financing with a motivated seller takes the gamble out of buying property.*

In the next chapter you will learn how to finance a property with little or no money down.

9

WHEN YOU HAVE LITTLE OR NO CASH TO PUT DOWN

A few people who should know better—seminar givers, real estate counselors, investment advisors, writers of real estate books—attempt to undermine our common sense and convince us that property can commonly be bought with no money down. Something for nothing! They tell us we can buy $100,000 or $1,000,000 properties without spending one dime. They should know better.

■ *CAUTION NOTE:* *Property cannot often be bought with no money down.*

As with many investment schemes—opportunities, as we learn in seminars—an element of truth exists. Occasionally we can buy expensive property with little or no money down. As we've seen, even a mortgage on a home can reach 90–95% of the selling price, minimizing a down payment.

■ *KEY POINT:* *Often you can buy property with 5–10% down.*

It's not that anything is wrong with a no-money-down deal. However, there are two stumbling blocks. The first is finding an owner who will agree to sell property to someone who is unable or unwilling to invest anything. The second is that a property is

157

difficult to pay for when financing is extremely high. Most income properties won't pay for themselves when fully financed.

■ *CAUTION NOTE: Obstacles to no-money-down deals include lack of a motivated seller and large mortgage payments.*

HOW TO GET STARTED WITH NO CASH

Despite our opening words of caution, we're going to examine various ways that do make sense to invest little or no cash as a down payment. There's no great mystery about it. To start, you need a highly motivated seller. You need his or her willingness to give you a purchase money mortgage for the entire purchase price, or secondary financing to make up the difference between a bank's first mortgage and the selling price.

■ *KEY POINT: Find a seller willing to arrange a no-money-down deal.*

Another alternative is to borrow the down payment from a third party, such as a commercial bank.

Nearly all of the techniques for buying with no money down involve instant money—mortgage money given by the seller. Most rely on the help of the seller. Negotiate with the seller, who will either give you the complete mortgage or extra financing beyond what the bank will loan.

■ *KEY POINT: Most no-money-down deals involve help from the seller.*

BUYING WITH NO MONEY DOWN

One way to do this without requiring the cooperation of the seller is to borrow the down payment from a commercial bank, not as a mortgage but as a personal loan. Banks are often willing to lend $5,000 on a signature, possibly more to individuals with a good financial history and the means to pay back the loan. Often they don't ask any questions about what the money is being used for. If they do, it is only out of concern that the money be used for a useful purpose, and what could be more useful than the purchase of real estate?

■ *KEY POINT: Commercial banks can often help out with personal, unsecured loans.*

Commercial banks can be found anywhere. These banks loan money to small businesses for inventory and goods, loan money to individuals for buying a car, and handle checking accounts. They often grant your loan request the same day, if not within 24 hours.

A more common way for investors to buy with no money down involves considerable help from the seller. It usually works best on investment or commercial property, since it requires a seller whose motivation to sell is strong.

Just because a seller must divest himself of a property doesn't mean it has any physical or economic problems. The seller may have held it too long, or maybe he's just tired of dealing with tenants or unable to make needed improvements.

■ *KEY POINT: Some sellers want to divest themselves of the property for intangible reasons.*

Most sellers of homes are unable to give 100% financing; some may not be able to give any at all. They may be moving to another area and need all the cash they can get to buy a new home. Or perhaps a couple is divorcing and it is impractical for them to hold a mortgage from a new buyer jointly.

■ *CAUTION NOTE: Not all sellers can help with financing, especially if they need all available cash to buy a new property.*

However, a businessperson with an investment is in a better position to negotiate the large amount of paper mortgage necessary for extensive financing.

■ *KEY POINT: Businesspersons owning income property are the best candidates to give extensive financing.*

Let's look at a no-money-down purchase where the seller makes up the difference between the new first mortgage and the selling price. The seller makes a deal with you for a price of $230,000 on a 12-unit apartment building. He presently has a mortgage of $80,000 on it. You tell him you want an all-cash, no-money-down deal. He is highly motivated to sell, and knows you could be a better manager of the property than he has been. He knows you would be a good risk, but he still needs to recover some cash from the deal.

You can't just take over the $80,000 mortgage and have the seller give you a second mortgage for the difference. He needs some cash or he won't sell it to you. Through negotiations, he agrees to the deal if he can put $40,000 in his pocket. You start by getting a $120,000 first mortgage at 13% interest. The old rate was 9%, and the bank, glad to have the opportunity to raise their rate and pleased that their exposure is only around 50% of the property's value, approves the loan the same day you present it to them.

Now the seller will get his $40,000 from the difference between the new mortgage of $120,000 and the $80,000 he must pay off on his old loan. He then gives you a second mortgage of $110,000, which, added to the new mortgage, equals the selling price. Since you accommodated his interest in getting cash via a new first mortgage, you negotiate with him a modest rate for his second mortgage: 11%, or two percentage points less than what you must pay on the first mortgage.

If, however, the seller had no existing mortgage, then he or she would be in a position to give you the whole mortgage. This is less common, since most investment properties carry existing financing.

■ *CAUTION NOTE: A seller can't give you a first mortgage on a property with existing financing.*

Almost any no-cash-down deal requires a motivated seller. He or she must be willing to take less cash and give huge secondary financing to make a deal. As the seminars tell you, find a seller who is distressed.

Psychology can help in a no-money-down sale. Most sellers are more interested in getting their asking price than they are in how the financing will work and how much cash they will get right away. This motivation may encourage the seller to deal in something other than cash. For example, if a seller's asking price is $230,000, they may be more willing to extend credit to a buyer who gives them the $230,000 on paper than to someone who offers $210,000 in cash.

■ *KEY POINT: Sellers often opt for a higher selling price on paper over a lesser offer in cash.*

This may not seem to make sense. As we saw in the last chapter, mortgages, that is, money pledged on paper, do tend to be worth less than their face value. We would rather have cash in hand than a promise to receive it in the future—unless there's a healthy interest rate attached to mollify our reluctance.

■ *KEY POINT: The interest rate compensates for the difference between the value of cash and a mortgage.*

However, sellers are emotional beings, distressed ones more so, and once a selling price is fixed in their mind, they'd rather negotiate on anything else before this amount. In fact, many buyers take advantage of this by offering the asking price or close to it, but on their terms. Often the only way you can meet a seller's price is to have much, if not all, of the transaction in notes and mortgages.

■ *KEY POINT: Start negotiating a no-money-down deal by offering the full price.*

The problem is that the entire, capital amount of the property is on paper, increasing indebtedness dramatically. If it's an apartment building, you may be worried about whether the rent money will cover the monthly payments. Whether it's one mortgage or broken up into four mortgages to as many different people, you will have a financial obligation of whopping proportions.

■ *CAUTION NOTE: The immense payments required by no-money-down transactions may not be covered by rental income.*

This doesn't mean these deals won't work; both the financing and the operation of the property can work. If it's an income property, look closely to make sure there's enough money from rents or be prepared to add a little each month.

WHEN IT'S BEST TO ADD A LITTLE

To avoid high payments, make some down payment. Any amount will help reduce monthly payments and bring them down to manageable proportions. A 100% financed deal in which every dollar beyond operating expenses goes out to meet mortgage indebtedness can lead to an unhealthy investment.

Even if you get a personal loan at a bank to help with the down payment, it still must be paid back. If you can put some down, it's money you don't have to come up with later.

In the beginning of a loan, interest is the bulk of the monthly payment. An actual reduction of the loan balance doesn't occur until years later.

Getting an unusually good deal from a seller might indicate a problem property. His problem might become your problem. If the property has deteriorated to the point that a tremendous capital investment is needed to keep it going, then you're defeating the purpose of putting no money down. You're going to need a lot of money to make these repairs.

■ *CAUTION NOTE:* *An anxious seller often indicates a distressed property needing capital expenditures.*

An owner may have been caught violating new zoning or health and safety regulations. The community or state then demands that these problems be fixed. If this requires a substantial and expensive upgrading of the property, this could make the owner become a seller.

■ *CAUTION NOTE:* *Having to meet new zoning or health and safety regulations can drive an owner to sell.*

In a problem-property sale, you, more often than not, are going to be the one who pays. Either the seller does the work and you pay more in sale price or you take over and spend the money yourself. Not that this is all bad. It's just that no-money-down deals often involve damaged properties. However, your awareness will be your protection when you are offered a no-money-down deal on a $150,000 property that's in bad shape—you can figure the deal at twice the price.

■ *KEY POINT:* *A distressed property can also mean you can negotiate a good deal.*

These distressed properties can frequently be good deals, but you must be knowledgeable and prepared to handle them financially. Sometimes when you put down some money, as little as a 5% down payment, you can get a much better property than one with 100% financing.

FIFTEEN WAYS TO BUY WITH LITTLE OR NO CASH

In this section, we'll discuss 15 ways in which you can buy a property with little or no money down.

Seller Financing For Low Down Payment. If the seller helps finance, you minimize your down payment. You often get a better deal from the seller than a bank. Neither a conventional nor ARM loan can match the benefits of seller financing.

Instead of 20% down, you can make deals only 5 or 10% down. The key is the seller's motivation. If strong enough, you can get a purchase money mortgage or a secondary mortgage for most of the selling price.

To encourage the seller, offer a higher rate of interest than the bank charges. If you don't have the cash, this often gets the property you want. The seller needn't be in dire straits to want to benefit from a little extra interest, particularly if you show good faith by putting down some down payment.

■ *KEY POINT: With the seller's help, you can minimize your down payment.*

Using Other Assets as Security. A blanket mortgage, also called an overlapping mortgage or trust deed, covers two or more separate parcels of property. Putting up a property you already own ensures you of getting a maximum amount of financing. With the risk spread over two or more properties, the blanket mortgage gives the lender some safety.

Blanket or overlapping mortgages also work if you obtain secondary financing from the seller. You pledge a second property, perhaps a house or business investment, as additional security for the second mortgage.

Either way, a blanket mortgage gives the bank or seller a margin of security, thereby guaranteeing you maximum financing.

■ *KEY POINT: A blanket mortgage overlapping other property gives the security needed to get a loan.*

Borrow on Other Property. A typical way to raise money is to borrow on presently owned property. This is not unlike the blanket mortgage.

Whether you want a second home or an investment, you can refinance your present mortgage. Sometimes the bank that holds the existing mortgage will add another mortgage as a second loan, giving you the money necessary for a down payment on another property—without taking any cash out of your pocket.

Naturally, you must already own a property with some minimal equity. However, if you have paid a mortgage on a home or small investment for several years, there should be enough equity for a bank to accept the property as additional security.

■ *KEY POINT: Extending your existing mortgage or borrowing a second raises the down payment for a new property.*

Enticing the Seller With Profit Sharing. If you have little or no down payment, promise the seller a share in either the property's income or future appreciation. Big banks and insurance companies do this in financing huge developments, so why not between private parties? The seller is more likely to provide full financing if there's hope for profit later.

Even banks have programs called shared-appreciation loans in which, for a minimal interest rate, they share in profits of the future sale of the property.

■ *KEY POINT: In a no-money-down deal, entice the seller with a share of the future profit.*

When Exchanging Property Can Be to Your Advantage. Bartering what we own is an age-old way of transferring assets, and there is nothing new about exchanging properties. We occasionally exchange homes and investors exchange income or commercial property, often in intricate two- three- and four-way deals. Each time we do so, we use our equity in the property being exchanged as leverage in getting new financing.

Exchanging property has special tax benefits for investors. If you sold an investment property, you would pay tax on the profit in the year of that sale—a profit based on your selling price minus any transaction costs and remaining tax basis (the original price of the property plus capital improvements minus depreciation taken). When you make an exchange of properties of equal value, you don't pay this tax. You defer it by the exchange, transferring your tax basis into the new property.

It is similar when you transfer your tax basis into a second residence. However, with a personal residence you don't have to make an actual exchange; you can sell and have up to 24 months to buy the new home. And as with investment property, you defer the tax on the profit.

You can keep repeating this process, but only if the property is a private residence. As long as you keep buying a property of the same or higher value, you can defer the tax on each gain until such time as you sell your final property without reinvesting.

But for investment property, exchange is the only way to avoid this tax. You can't sell and find something else—the second property must be part of the exchange. However, depending on the value of the properties, you benefit by minimizing the need for a substantial down payment.

The combination of minimal down payment and low taxes makes this technique popular for professional real estate investors, who even form clubs that actively seek owners with whom they can make exchanges.

■ *KEY POINT: When you exchange one property for another, your present equity is used as the down payment.*

Government Veterans Administration Loans.   If you are a veteran, you can purchase a home with no down payment if the home is appraised to within acceptable limits.

These so-called GI loans are fraught with paperwork and constantly changing regulations. Banks, which are involved in lending the money, shy away from these loans when the stated rate at which they must lend the money is less than that of their fixed rate loans. The banks do, however, get a guarantee from the government which protects them in case of default.

If you qualify, you can buy an approved home with no down payment.

■ *KEY POINT: If you qualify for a GI loan, you can buy with no down payment.*

Federal Housing Administration Guarantee.   FHA loans, like GI loans, are not made by the government. Institutional lenders loan the money, and the FHA insures them against loss. The rates vary with market conditions.

The advantage is that the down payment may be less than with a conventional loan; often the loans can be up to 97% of the property's appraised value. The FHA has an intricate appraisal process with high standards that protects you from paying an excessive price.

■ *KEY POINT: Although time-consuming, a FHA loan minimizes the down payment to 3%.*

Private Mortgage Insurance.   Privately owned companies, often branches or subsidiaries of large insurance companies, are active in guaranteeing mortgages. Guarantees have become popular with banks in the last decade. They take the burden off the bank in case of default.

Here's how it works. A borrower pays an extra quarter or half a percent in interest as a fee for insurance to a private insurer in addition to the regular interest. In case of default, this insurance company will reimburse the lending bank a portion of the loan, thus protecting the bank against an entire loss. The bank is therefore in a safer position to lend a higher percentage of loan to property value—90% rather than 80%—than they would otherwise.

With some banks you can buy a home with only 5% down with a guarantee from a private mortgage company.

■ *KEY POINT: For a fee of ½%, you can buy mortgage insurance, minimizing the down payment to 5–10%.*

Lease With Option.   Discussed in the last chapter, this technique has many variations. One is to minimize your down payment or initial investment in the property.

Whether you lease or manage the property, your control over the property begins immediately—often without any down payment.

In some cases, a seller will want some money down to show good faith, but not always. After all, you are simply leasing or managing the property with the promise that at some future date you will take title. Perhaps you won't actually take title until you have found a buyer you wish to sell it to.

It's a way not only to buy control of a property now, but to defer financing it until later, when the increase of the property's value will make mortgage money easier to get.

■ *KEY POINT: Leasing with option may only require a minimal down payment to secure the option.*

Management Agreement With Option.   This is similar to the lease with option to buy except it usually involves a larger purchase. You wouldn't think of managing a home and then purchasing later, but you might lease it with the promise that you will take title later.

The management agreement with option might be used for an investment where the present owner doesn't want to relinquish control until he or she is satisfied with your performance. If you were acquiring an apartment complex or shopping center from an institutional owner such as an insurance company from whom you'll also receive financing, the deal might be conditional upon your success on the job.

Properties such as apartment buildings or commercial ventures often demand your active participation. They need management from an executive perspective. In taking over this way, you'll be in a similar position as the seller. Under a strict management arrangement, being a property manager means making the decisions. The seller may not even come on the property, perhaps only meeting with you occasionally for information.

If the deal is large and complex and you want to take over but need experience and a chance to build credit, the gradual takeover of a management agreement with option to buy may be right for you. You gain control with a minimal down payment, if any at all, as well as experience in running it (dealing with tenants, vendors, etc.) before you actually take title.

But perhaps its biggest benefit is that you arrange for a purchase price in today's market that won't have to be paid until a time in the future—making it easier for you to finance the deal.

■ *KEY POINT: As in leasing, a management agreement with option to buy may require only a small down payment to hold the option.*

Borrow From Relatives.   A person starting out can some-times get a little help from parents or relatives. A few thousand dollars, either as an outright gift or as a loan with a minimal in-terest rate, might be just enough help for a down payment.

If, you don't own any property but wish to buy your first, often you'll find relatives willing to come to your aid. Some-times they got their start that way and now that they have some money are glad to help. Perhaps you don't need much because you're able to put in some yourself. You would be surprised at the number of buyers who turn to their relatives to borrow the down payment. The first family home is often bought with such help.

■ *KEY POINT: Family will often extend a low-interest loan to help with the down payment.*

Getting a Seller to Pay Your Closing Costs.   Aside from giving the mortgage itself, a seller can help you by paying the closing costs. This amount, depending on the type of loan and property, can be substantial.

The costs include your lawyer's fee, the title search required by the bank, transfer fees required by the Registry of Deeds, and, most costly of all, any points you might incur upon origi-nating the mortgage.

You may wonder why the seller would want to pay these costs. The answer is motivation. If the seller is anxious, he or she will consider it to swing the deal. If you've got just enough cash for the down payment and are unable to come up with closing costs, the seller may very likely accept this burden. You could also borrow the money from the seller by signing a short-term note and reimbursing him later.

In Veterans Administration financing, the seller is required to pay both points and any escrow fees. If eligible for a VA loan, you could buy a house with absolutely no down payment and no closing costs. However, be aware that selling price or terms of financing may be adjusted to make up this difference. Unfortunately, sellers often boost the selling price unfairly in these situations.

■ *KEY POINT: An anxious seller may pay or loan you money for closing costs, minimizing the funds needed to buy.*

Buy Out Equity on Property About to Be Foreclosed.   Similar to buying a foreclosed property from a bank is buying directly from an owner whose property is being foreclosed. In most areas, foreclosures are not common, but occasionally people default on their loans.

The seller in financial difficulty or about to default is usually willing to get out from under the heavy payments by having someone take them over and taking a second mortgage for his equity. Taking over this person's loan, with no down payment, can be an excellent deal. You could also negotiate a take-over with the bank that holds the existing loan to arrange for more money or a second mortgage to free the seller completely.

A property owner about to default can own anything from a single-family home to a huge apartment complex. You can find out who's in trouble from the local banks or real estate agents. Before foreclosing on a property, a bank must advertise their intent in the local newspaper. That may give you several weeks to make a deal.

Taking over a property about to be foreclosed is often done in conjunction with the bank that holds the mortgage. It offers you easy financing with hardly any down payment and relieves the seller of his financial obligation. Lenders don't like to foreclose, so any reasonable arrangement will stop them.

■ *KEY POINT: The seller about to default is motivated to help with financing.*

Buy Foreclosed Property From Bank. Sometimes properties are foreclosed and become the inventory of a bank. The properties can be houses, investments, apartments, condominiums, land, or commercial blocks. They arrive on the foreclosed list because owners, builders, or developers have defaulted on their loans. You can take advantage of this situation.

Most banks do not try to profit in this situation; they just want what money they have invested in the property. You can often get a property at less than open-market prices. If a bank has a substantial amount of money invested in a property, it will often sell to any qualified buyer for the amount of financing, or 100%.

Not only will you get a discount in buying a foreclosed property, but you can take over without putting up much money. A bank might require some money down to ensure your interest, but even this would be a formality.

Whether you are seeking a home or investment, talk to banks about what properties they have in their portfolio. You will find you can arrange a modest purchase price as well as favorable terms on a loan.

■ *KEY POINT: Once the foreclosed property is owned by the bank, you can often take over for the balance of the liability.*

Take in Partners. Americans are not used to buying property in groups, but this can be a good idea. We work together in other ways, so why not in this way?

You can buy a larger property by pooling your assets with another investor. You stretch your down payment and have more credit to sign for a larger loan.

Partnerships often work in real estate because the investment is basically a static one. Unless you're building, it doesn't usually require daily involvement. You're not in a store selling toasters or pork. You own a property that will make money for you day or night. The beauty of real estate investment is that it doesn't demand ongoing involvement except at particular times. You make money while you sleep, and this is even more true of partnerships.

Many real estate partnerships have formed over the years, small ones with a group of friends, or large, limited partnerships of 25–500 people sponsored by investment companies. Either way, a partnership benefits you by minimizing your down payment while securing a property of considerable size, one inherently more profitable than any you could buy alone.

■ *KEY POINT:* *Buying with one or more partners allows you to pool funds and take over a larger property*

THE DO'S AND DON'T'S OF BUYING WITH LITTLE OR NO MONEY DOWN

The biggest problem in buying a property with little or no down payment is that its condition will probably be undesirable. At first you may be attracted by favorable financing and a low purchase price. But such properties, commonly income properties, become distressed because they have problems.

Be wary. If the property is working well—if there's enough money to meet operating expenses and mortgage payments and still have some left over—there is usually no reason for the seller to accept anything less than the most advantageous deal.

■ *CAUTION NOTE:* *When the seller will finance 100%, the property may have physical or economic problems.*

Examine the property carefully. Find out why the seller wants out. The property may need extensive repair. Physical deterioration might be causing delayed rental payments from tenants. Meeting new zoning or building code violations might be prohibitively expensive.

Have a local building inspector give you a report on his findings.

■ *CAUTION NOTE:*   *Inspect no-money-down property thoroughly.*

Sometimes no-money-down property is beyond saving. Unwary buyers enticed by dreams of making money in real estate have been caught in financial disasters. So put down a little money, as much down payment as you can manage, and get a better property.

■ *KEY POINT:*   *You can often buy a property by putting down some cash.*

Another problem in minimizing the down payment is handling the numerous mortgages simultaneously. Your monthly payments may be excessive. If it's an investment property, then you must be sure that you have enough income from the property or additional resources to meet these obligations. If you buy a fully financed, single-family home to live in, your wages must be sufficient to pay the mortgages.

■ *CAUTION NOTE:*   *Fully financed properties mean heavy mortgage payments.*

However, owning property is one of the fastest ways to build equity and save money for the future. If you need a home or an investment and only have a minimal down payment, this must be the way to do it. You've got to get started some time. The admonitions here give you some guidelines.

Properties whose owners are highly motivated to sell are not always a bad deal. You should just be careful; you don't want a seller's distress to become your nightmare.

■ *KEY POINT: Being careful in a no-money-down deal is the best way to get the right property.*

In the next chapter we will explore the many tax advantages of financing and owning real estate.

INNOVATIVE TECHNIQUES FOR CREATIVE FINANCING **10**

In the last few years, many new loan formats have been introduced, but the truth is, most of them are simply varieties of existing loan formats.

Many experts on the consumer side of mortgage banking wonder why borrowers should see anything other than the conventional fixed rate, 30-year mortgage as being the best for them. In truth, they are partly right. Part of the problem is that banks hedge their bets on mortgages by promoting adjustable rate loans. This protects them but doesn't always show concern for the consumer. However, it is possible in certain situations to find mortgages that benefit the borrower. Many of them discussed in this chapter are a variation of the fixed rate or the adjustable rate loan with a convertible option.

■ *KEY POINT: Many loan formats are variations of fixed rate and adjustable rate loans.*

CONVERTING EQUITY THROUGH A REVERSE MORTGAGE

A reverse mortgage is a way you can transform a property that has substantial value into cash, without selling the property or refinancing. It is a form of refinancing that eliminates the burdensome problem of monthly payments.

■ *KEY POINT: A reverse mortgage allows you to turn equity into cash without giving up ownership.*

Many people—perhaps those who have lost a spouse or who are contemplating retirement—who don't want to leave their home and neighborhood but need some financial help, turn to a reverse mortgage that will pay them a certain amount of money each month to cover taxes, utility costs, medical bills, and personal expenses, and so forth.

A reverse mortgage pays a borrower a fixed monthly amount and defers repayment. It can be done through an Individual Reverse Mortgage Account (IRMA), in which the lender receives all or part of the value of the home, including appreciation during the term of its loan, in return for deferring repayment until the borrower decides to move or passes away. Upon the borrower's death, the estate pays off the debt.

Although there are approximately 2 to 3% closing costs with a typical reverse mortgage, the income you get from it depends on its size and, to a certain extent, the life expectancy of you and your spouse. If you live long, your payments from a reverse mortgage may exceed the value of the equity; if you die before equity in the property is used up, your estate must repay the lender the money you gained, with interest, plus all or a portion of the appreciation that has been gained since the mortgage was first taken out.

■ *KEY POINT: A reverse mortgage pays the borrower money in regular monthly payments.*

Again, this works well for people over sixty who have property of substantial value they want to turn into cash. Note that the funds from the reverse mortgage do not go to pay someone from whom you are purchasing property, but go to you, not in one lump sum amount, but in regular monthly intervals.

The danger in a reverse mortgage is that eventually the loan must be repaid or the property reverts to the full ownership and control of the lender. However, occasionally these loans do make sense, particularly if a person is infirm, and perhaps in need of home health care or the services of a nursing home, where large expenses are anticipated.

■ *CAUTION NOTE: Although a reverse mortgage converts equity to cash payments to you, it may mean eventual loss of ownership.*

The reverse mortgage, then, is a way in which equity in your house can be converted into regular income. It should be approached with caution, and only with the advice of an attorney and tax accountant.

THE PRICE-LEVEL ADJUSTED MORTGAGE (PLAM)

A PLAM is a fully amortizing loan with a long-term payoff, whose monthly payments are structured to be constant in purchasing power over the life of the loan. The initial payments on the mortgage are computed as if for a long, fixed rate loan, at the prevailing real rate of interest adjusted for inflation. Sound complex? It is, but it does mean much lower monthly payments in the early years.

Here's how it works: take a $100,000, 30-year mortgage. With a PLAM at 5%, the first year's monthly payments would be just under $540. With a fixed rate mortgage at a current rate of around 12%, the monthly payments would be close to $1,030. Even counting in the deductibility of mortgage interest, the difference in monthly payments is huge, making the PLAM much more affordable, particularly for a young couple starting out.

■ *KEY POINT: PLAM means lower payments at the beginning of the loan.*

What PLAM does is protect the lender against inflation, because the principal amount of the mortgage based on a particular inflation rate rises accordingly. For example, at 10% inflation, the $100,000 mortgage will actually increase to $110,000 at the end of the year. In theory this increase in debt is offset by the potential appreciation in the property. The gamble is that the property will increase in value as fast, if not faster, than this negative amortization increases the debt. In addition, it is hoped that the homeowner's income will increase in order to pay this extra amount.

■ *CAUTION NOTE: The principal balance of the PLAM loan rises along with inflation.*

It is a tradeoff: You as a borrower get lower monthly payments, whereas the lender gets his capital protected against the unexpected higher cost of inflation. With PLAM, you do not gamble on what the future will hold. It is constantly adjusted to whatever the rate of inflation is. The idea is to remove the vicissitudes of inflation from the interest rate.

The advantages to a PLAM are that, to a degree, it satisfies the needs of both parties. The borrowers want low payments, and the lenders want their investment back, plus interest, adjusted for what inflation took away. The outstanding balance of the loan is adjusted each month for inflation. Housing and urban development economists recommend that the urban Consumer Price index be used for these adjustments.

Is this type of loan similar to the adjustable rate mortgages that lenders have been anxious to lend out? Adjustable rate mortgages are typically tied to short-term interest rates, such as the one-year Treasury bill, whereas PLAMs are usually adjusted for inflation using the Consumer Price index. The difference between an adjustable rate loan and a PLAM is important, too. The underlying principal balance of a PLAM is adjusted, not the interest rate.

■ *KEY POINT:*   *The principal balance of the loan is adjusted, not the interest rate.*

The idea behind this is that the Consumer Price index is going to fluctuate less wildly than the interest rate on one-year Treasury bills. For example, the interest rate on an adjustable rate mortgage rising two points, say from 8 to 10%, could cause an increase in monthly payments on a 30-year, $100,000 loan from $734 a month to $878 a month. That is a large increase, particularly if you are just meeting the payments prior to the increase. With a PLAM, in the early years of a $100,000 loan, the increase would only be $60 or $70.

One of the drawbacks of a PLAM is that people don't get a sense that they will ever own their own home, and it is true. Substantial amounts of equity are pledged to the lender as time goes on in the loan. In a sense, it is similar to the home equity loan, where you take a fair amount of equity and use it for other expenses. From a lender's point of view, this is an ideal way to lend money, as changes in the price level during the term of the loan are reflected not only in larger payments on the loan, but also in the outstanding balance, giving the lender a big bonus at the end of the term.

■ *CAUTION NOTE:*   *A PLAM may be unfairly advantageous to the lender, as additional equity becomes automatically pledged as inflation rises.*

One of the biggest problems with PLAMs is finding borrowers who want to gamble on this type of financing. Although much discussed, it will take time to see if PLAMs achieve any popularity. But for people who need a mortgage with payments of $500, rather than $1,000 a month, this may be the way to go.

TWENTY-FIVE WAYS TO FINANCE ANY PROPERTY

Conventional Mortgages. In the conventional fixed rate mortgage, monthly payments are set at the time you begin the loan. They are based on the overall money borrowed, the interest rate, and the number of years until the loan balance is paid off.

Interest rate and term of loan offer you flexibility. The lower the interest rate and amount borrowed, the lower the monthly payment. A shorter period allows you to pay the loan off more rapidly.

Interest rates vary from one source to another. The conventional fixed rate mortgage is commonly available not only from banks, but also from alternative sources: credit unions, trust funds, and even the seller.

■ *KEY POINT: Conventional fixed rate loans are available from many sources.*

Adjustable Rate Mortgages (ARM). In this mortgage, discussed fully in Chapter 7, payments fluctuate in amount because the interest rate varies according to a specifically chosen national indicator which may rise or fall over the life of the mortgage. An ARM is normally available only from institutional lenders.

An ARM usually starts at a slightly lower interest rate than a conventional fixed rate mortgage. The bank wants you to borrow this way because in an ARM the responsibility of shouldering the long-term effect of a rising interest rate is shifted from the bank to the borrower. The bank feels it will have greater security lending through ARMs, since the borrower must pay more if rates go up.

However, if you want to gamble that interest rates will go down from the time you borrow, an ARM might be the best arrangement for you. You must decide if the lack of security (security provided by the constant payment of the fixed rate mortgage) bothers you. It is a little like horse racing. If you feel the lower interest rate will win out, that is the one to bet on.

■ *KEY POINT:* *The interest rate in an ARM fluctuates according to a national economic indicator.*

Second and Third Mortgages.   A common way for a seller to help a buyer is to offer a second mortgage. It's the oldest form of creative financing. This money is borrowed over and above the amount of the first mortgage: for example, you borrow 80% of the property's selling price from a bank, and the seller, being motivated, gives you another 10–15% as a loan. Often the holding period for a second mortgage is shorter than what you might get with a conventional or adjustable rate loan (five to ten years compared with twenty or thirty, for example).

■ *KEY POINT:* *A second mortgage is a fixed rate loan over and above the first mortgage.*

Second mortgages are common in financing investment property. Here, a buyer often assumes an existing mortgage that might be low compared with the current selling price. For example, in assuming a loan of 50% of value, most buyers don't have or aren't willing to put up another 50% as a down payment. To make the deal, it is not unreasonable for the seller to offer another 40% as a second mortgage. The terms and interest rate may be similar to what a bank would charge for new money, but it allows you to purchase at a nominal 10% cash. And you have the benefit of the assumed loan with its lower rate.

■ *KEY POINT:* *Second mortgages are usually given by the seller to minimize the buyer's down payment.*

A second or third mortgage should only under special circumstances be negotiated with a quick payoff. Having to pay off a large sum within a year or two might strap you financially.

It can work, however, if you are expecting some cash, such as an inheritance, to come your way when the amount is due. For example, let's say you buy a home and the seller furnishes the first $5,000 of the purchase price without any repayment required from you until the following year. That may be fine to get you into the house, but may endanger your chances of keeping it if you are forced to come up with a lump-sum payment that could be beyond your means.

■ *CAUTION NOTE: Plan for additional funds when second mortgages have quick payoffs.*

Normally, structure a second or third mortgage like a conventional loan with fixed interest rate and monthly, quarterly, or semiannual payments—payments that can be made out of your income or cash from your investment.

Seller Financing.   Seller financing is the easiest way to create instant money. In effect, the seller loans you equity he or she already has in the property and receives that equity back in the form of payments based on a negotiated interest rate over a period of time until the full amount of this equity is paid off.

■ *KEY POINT: Seller financing means a purchase is made with part or all of the mortgage funds coming from the seller's equity.*

Seller financing is similar to a bank giving you a first mortgage (eg, 80–90% of the property's value as a loan), but instead it is given by the seller.

■ *KEY POINT: Most seller financing is in the form of conventional fixed rate loans.*

There are numerous ways to create seller financing, often called creative financing. More ways are explained in Chapter 6. However, in buying any property, you should always consider

having the seller give you back a mortgage at terms more advantageous than you could get from an institutional source.

■ *KEY POINT: In buying property always consider asking the seller
for financing.*

Purchase Money Mortgages. A purchase money mortgage
is a first mortgage financed by the seller. Often referred to by
different names, it is the most common way for a seller to help
a buyer. These mortgages are usually fixed rate loans with constant payments.

In a purchase money mortgage, a portion, if not all, of the
money used to purchase the property is in the form of a mortgage
held by the seller. It might be a first, second, or third mortgage.

■ *KEY POINT: Purchase money mortgages are first mortgages given
by the seller.*

Assumed Mortgages. When a loan is transferred from a
seller to a buyer, it is called a mortgage assumption. The buyer
assumes the obligation to pay the old mortgage based on the
old mortgage's interest rate and remaining term.

Since the balance of the assumed mortgage has been reduced
by payments over the time it has been held, it may be relatively
low in relation to the current selling price. Additional financing
is usually necessary when a loan is assumed.

■ *KEY POINT: Assuming a mortgage is taking over a seller's loan
balance.*

The purpose of assuming a mortgage is to take over a low-
interest loan. Banks don't like you to assume one of their loans.
For years, they have stipulated in their agreements that a second
borrower cannot take over a loan. However, if this clause is not
in the agreement (consult with your lawyer), you may save yourself a considerable amount of cash.

Some court decisions state that banks must allow these take-overs. Sometimes banks will allow them if they can pass a favorable judgment on your credit-worthiness. In giving you permission to take over, they sometimes even release the previous borrower from his liability on the loan.

■ *CAUTION NOTE: Many loans are not assumable.*

In most cases, however, assuming the mortgage means taking the mortgage "subject to" loan, where you're simply taking over the loan payment without negotiation with the original mortgage lender. This is a matter to discuss with your lawyer or real estate agent to see what the prevailing banking practices in your area are and what laws may affect the assumption of the mortgage.

When possible, it is an excellent way to finance. As we saw in the first chapter, the balance on relatively recent loans does not decrease until the later stages of the loan and can thus take many years. In the first five or ten years of an assumed mortgage, still a fair amount of principal can be paid off.

Government FHA Loans.   Federal Housing Administration loans vary in availability and the amount of money one can borrow from time to time. Different programs are sponsored by the FHA. Some programs give money directly; others guarantee to a local lender the repayment of that money. Most guarantee a lower interest rate. This benefit is sometimes lessened by the lender charging points to originate the loan. A good bit of paperwork slows down the purchase process. The FHA is not the place to get a quick commitment.

■ *KEY POINT: Although FHA loan commitments are slow, they allow low down payments.*

Government VA Guarantee.   A government Veterans Administration guarantee is similar to the FHA loan, but you must be a veteran. Called the GI loan, it also limits the amount you can finance. The loans are given for homes only. Whereas the FHA insists upon a minimal down payment, the VA loan can require no down payment unless the loan amount is over a particular limit. Again, points can be charged by the institutional lender and terms and conditions of the loan manipulated by them.

Consider this route if you are a veteran and buying your first home.

■ *KEY POINT:*   *Little or no down payment is necessary for a GI loan if you are a veteran.*

Lease With Option to Buy.   Any time you're short of cash for a down payment, you can lease a property with an option to buy it at a later time. This gives you a way to take over use of the property without the full cost of ownership. You don't even have to talk to the bank. Financing will come later when you exercise your option.

Rarely do you have to make a full down payment to take over. Often, only 1–5% of the agreed-upon price will suffice for the option.

The lease with option gives you time to investigate the property before buying. Often used by professional investors, it is a readily adaptable device. It may be used to take over a parcel of land upon which you might wish to build or a house on which the seller is willing to defer the closing.

This method is thoroughly explained in Chapter 8.

■ *KEY POINT:*   *The lease with option to buy allows you to control the property while deferring the purchase decision.*

Management Agreement With Option to Buy.   Here's another way to take over a property while deferring purchase and financing. It is a way to take control with no down payment except what monies might be advanced for securing the option with the seller.

It is the same as the lease with option to buy except that your control of property is greater. You are the manager, essentially taking the place of the seller. If, for example, the property is a commercial building with tenants, they must report and pay their rent to you. In turn, you accept the responsibilities of the owner in dealing with their needs.

The management agreement with option to buy, like the lease with option to buy, allows a period of time in which to become familiar with the property before purchasing. More on this unique way of taking control of a property in Chapter 8.

■ *KEY POINT: The management agreement with option to buy puts you in the position of ownership before actually purchasing.*

Sale–Leaseback.   Some investors shop for opportunities to take over property in a sale–leaseback. These deals usually involve an established single tenant, such as a fast food chain or an automobile dealership.

Often, a business that has owned and occupied a commercial property for a number of years, having depreciated it for tax purposes, finds benefit in selling the building, getting the cash for it, and remaining there as a tenant. It is an easy deal for you to negotiate, and you end up with the property and a tenant who is the former owner.

■ *KEY POINT: A sale–leaseback is usually a property bought from a seller who remains as a tenant.*

In some cases the seller may give you a mortgage that fully finances the purchase. Often you can buy this way with a minimal down payment.

■ *KEY POINT: Sale–leasebacks are often financed by the seller.*

You then have an investment in which all mortgage costs and expenses are paid for by the rent. You are also able to take the building (not the land) portion of the property based on the current sale price and make depreciation deductions. These are discussed in Chapter 13.

Why does the original owner want to do this? Simple. He's going to get a lot of cash from you in the form of a mortgage plus any down payment that you might give him—cash that he can now use to buy equipment to make more hamburgers or Frisbees. And, almost as important, he can now deduct his rent payments, where previously he had used up his (taxable) depreciable assets.

A sale–leaseback is an excellent type of arrangement to make as a joint venture or partnership with other investors. As with any purchasing or financing arrangement, a knowledgeable attorney with a specialty in taxes should structure the investment.

■ *KEY POINT:* *Sale–leasebacks usually involve other investors.*

Trade-in Property or Chattel Goods. One way to reduce the need for a down payment is for a willing seller to take payment in other than cash. An automobile, boat, stocks or bonds, or even other real estate such as a vacation home or parcel of land could be accepted by the seller as part of the deal.

Stocks and bonds have a specific value easily verified by a seller. This saves you the burden of having to sell the stock and pay taxes on it.

More often than you would think, a seller of home or investment property will accept a car or even a boat. It may seem odd, but generally any sale boils down to the seller's motivation. If it's strong enough, they're likely to accept chattel goods. Sometimes sellers, in a strong desire to change and move on, just want out.

■ *KEY POINT:* *Down payments can often be tangible goods such as cars or boats, or anything the seller might accept.*

Exchanging Property.   Exchanging property is trading one property for another. Usually, one investment property for another is what is known as a "like-kind" exchange.

It is a way to defer taxes by transferring one's tax consequence into the second property. The tax on your profit is not paid until this second property is sold. Investors who specialize in exchanging keep their profits moving through several trades before they pay a tax.

Exchanging is considered one of the fastest ways to build equity in real estate. More on this in Chapter 8.

■ *KEY POINT: Great fortunes can be made in trading one property for another.*

The Wraparound Mortgage.   The wraparound mortgage, or all-inclusive mortgage, is all of the existing first, second, and third mortgages plus the addition on any new money loaned by a lender. The mortgage then "wraps around" the existing mortgages.

The wraparound is an excellent technique when the existing mortgages have a low interest rate and are unassumable. There'll be more on this excellent tool of financing property in Chapter 8.

■ *KEY POINT: The wraparound allows you to take over existing financing by making an overall mortgage with the seller.*

Commercial or Personal Loans.   You don't always have to negotiate formal mortgages at a bank to borrow the money needed to purchase. With a purchase money mortgage from the seller, a personal or business loan from a commercial bank can make up the down payment.

Banks that lend money in the form of personal loans aren't fussy as in the past about what the money is for. Often, that extra $5,000 or $10,000 needed to make a deal can be obtained with just your signature—without all the appraisals or signing of papers.

■ *KEY POINT:* *A commercial or personal loan can be used as a down payment.*

Usually, you must have previously established good credit to get a personal loan. Some establish credit by borrowing money, putting it in a savings account, and then paying it back when it is due. Often, the only security for the bank is your good faith in making payments.

In some areas you don't need as exemplary a credit history for getting a $70,000 mortgage on a house or commercial property as you do in borrowing $5,000 in the form of a personal loan. This happens, in part, because the property itself is the security for the mortgage, while only your ability to pay is the security for the personal loan.

Limited Partnership. A limited partnership is a group of investors pooling their money for the purpose of investment. A general partner controls the enterprise. A commercial or residential development, whether an existing or a new property, could be the investment.

A limited partnership benefits you, as a limited partner, because you become part owner of a property larger than you could purchase on your own. Also, you don't participate directly in the arrangement for the mortgage; a general partner negotiates the financing.

■ *KEY POINT:* *Combining your funds with other investors' funds in a limited partnership allows purchase of a larger investment.*

Whether the group involves six or six hundred people, you will "own" a respective amount of equity in proportion to the total equity of the property, including a proportionate share of the property's mortgage. For example, if you invest $10,000 along with 99 other investors, you have $1,000,000, which as a down payment buys a $5,000,000 property, $4,000,000 of which is financed, perhaps by a group of large mortgage banks or an insurance company.

You put $10,000 of equity into the property plus a "share" of the mortgage of $40,000. You didn't have to go out and negotiate or commit yourself personally for this mortgage. The net effect of your $10,000 buys a $50,000 deal, just as if you bought a house for $50,000 and put $10,000 down.

A limited partnership is an excellent way to purchase a larger investment than you would normally negotiate on your own and be free of the property's management. The general partner runs the partnership. However, as many investors have found out, the strength of these investments is only as good as the property that the partnership controls. Too high an original purchase price, exorbitant brokerage fees, or unreasonable commissions for the continued management of the project have soured some investments. But if entered into wisely, with full knowledge of the property and the aims of the partnership and general partner, limited partnerships can be an excellent way to finance and own property.

■ *CAUTION NOTE: A limited partnership is only as good as the property it buys.*

Life Estate.   An unusual way to purchase with unique benefits for both the buyer and seller is commonly known as the life estate purchase. Although this type of transaction has different forms, normally a seller becomes a tenant in his or her own house. For example, a seller, perhaps an older person lacking dependents or an adequate income to sustain her over the remaining years of her life, sells her property to an investor but remains a tenant. She gives a mortgage, accepting a minimal down payment. She will receive monthly payments based on an annuity running for the remaining time of her life.

In effect, the seller has her house, continues to live in it, and receives an income without the burden of rent or property taxes. The investor gambles that the value of the property will grow.

■ *KEY POINT: In a life estate purchase, a seller who gives the mortgage remains as a tenant for life.*

What is the source of money you need to give the seller each month for property you don't have use of and cannot rent out? This arrangement is commonly negotiated so that payments to the seller are based on an annuity factored by the projected remaining years of that person's life. For example, if you as the investor, gamble that this person will live 10 more years, you will expect to pay monthly payments for that 10-year period. Factored into these payments is a reasonable interest rate that is based on the 10-year term.

This may not seem like a mortgage, but computations of the monthly payments are similar. You, as the investor, own the property. To make it work financially for you, mortgage the property with a bank, reinvest this money in a safe, insured manner, and, in turn, make payments to the bank and to the seller.

As you can see, the life estate method has advantages for both buyer and seller. The seller gets a lifetime annuity for a property based on today's value.

Tomorrow's value to the seller is unimportant, since no one can spend money after they're dead. And if the seller outlives the original projection of his or her remaining years (the payments having been based on such figures from an annuity table), he or she can thereby receive more money than what the original "mortgage" was expected to be. In addition to this income, the seller retains possession of his or her home.

The advantage for you as an investor is that you didn't have to put down much money to acquire the property, a property that will increase in value with little effort on your part. However, you must be cautious. The stream of money needed to make payments to the seller, now your tenant, can be difficult to find. And, as discussed, the seller may live longer than anticipated, holding up eventual possession of the property. But if you can arrive at a satisfactory payment plan, it can provide a big bonus for you in the future.

■ *CAUTION NOTE:*   *Sellers can remain as life tenants for a long time.*

Refinance on Purchase.   The refinance on purchase technique is taking possession of a property and then refinancing the property for more than the original loans you assumed or placed. You do this to gain back some of the equity or cash down payment you placed on it. It can be done to get out from under a short-term second mortgage, meet a large payment deadline, or simply put some cash in your pocket.

A typical way to use this technique is to wait some minimal time, perhaps a year after purchase, after you have made improvements and the property has increased in value. Often, a bank is willing to increase its commitment on the mortgage. These are not difficult loans to get if the bank is convinced there has been a change in value and the total amount of their mortgage does not seem excessive to them.

■ *KEY POINT:*   *Refinance on purchase is asking the bank for more money after you take title.*

Borrow on Equity.   Borrowing on equity is similar to the refinance on purchase except that you have a substantial amount of equity which you may wish to either put in your pocket or use as security for another mortgage.

Both savings banks and commercial banks can be approached to refinance your equity. They don't always have to be secured by an official mortgage instrument, as the equity could be given to you in the form of a personal loan. Or, a commercial bank, even a savings bank, can negotiate second mortgages beyond an existing first, thus releasing equity money to you.

■ *KEY POINT: Once you have equity, you can refinance.*

Blanket Mortgage.   This mortgage covers more than one property. It is ideal when you buy a second home, for example, a vacation home. You put up the security of your present home, or other property, as security for the new property.

You may think, "Well, why isn't the second home a security in itself?" True, you won't have to merge the two properties in one mortgage in most cases. Commonly, though, the second or vacation home is in another area, perhaps another state, and banks get worried about lending money for properties in areas they are not familiar with. The equity in your present home serves as security for what becomes an overall blanket loan on both properties. It can often make the deal, especially when you are buying in another area.

■ *KEY POINT: In a blanket mortgage, your present property acts as security for an overall loan covering a new, additional property.*

Contract for Deed.   The contract for deed, or land sales contract, has varying names in different areas of the country. This is another technique used when it is impossible to take over existing financing or when no financing exists at all, and you wish to make only a small down payment. Here the seller retains legal title to the property.

In a contract for deed, the seller gives you a large balance in the form of a mortgage but retains title to the property until the mortgage or "contract" is paid off. The deed is usually held in escrow and recorded only upon the final payoff.

■ *KEY POINT: In the contract for deed, the seller gives the financing and holds the deed in escrow until the mortgage is paid off.*

This type of purchase is similar to the management agreement with option to buy in that it is issued when present financing is difficult. However, it is used by the homeowner instead of an investor.

The seller benefits by making the sale when money is tight and interest rates are high. You benefit by purchasing at a negotiated, lower interest rate and down payment. The seller feels secure in the sale since he or she still holds legal title to the property in case of default.

A contract for deed, or land sales contract, was more popular in the past and is not used as much today. However, it is still a valid financing device for you to buy a property when financing is difficult.

■ *KEY POINT: The contract for deed technique is commonly used only when new financing is scarce.*

Trust Deeds.   In using a trust deed to purchase, you get a mortgage from the seller after a nominal down payment. The seller then signs the deed, which is held in trust until such time as the mortgage has been fully paid.

Similar to the contract for deed, it is used when the seller must finance because of a lack of existing mortgage money.

■ *KEY POINT: In a trust deed, the seller gives the mortgage and holds the deed until it is paid off.*

Trust Deed With Balloon Payment.   The trust deed with balloon payment is similar to the trust deed except that at some future time a "balloon" payment is made on the mortgage, either reducing it substantially or paying it off entirely. At this time, the deed is released from escrow and given to you for recording.

The trust deed with balloon payment encourages a seller to give financing, as he or she will be paid off (in a shorter amount of time than under other agreements) when the mortgage "balloons."

■ *KEY POINT:* *The trust deed with balloon payment can convince a seller to finance for a short time.*

■ *CAUTION NOTE:* *Future funds must be provided for to meet balloon provisions in mortgages.*

Repurchase Option.   The repurchase option is a way to sell a property that you own while retaining the right to repurchase it at some future time. It is a guarantee that you can regain the use of an asset that, for a temporary period, you don't need.

■ *KEY POINT:* *The repurchase option allows you to sell now and rebuy later.*

The repurchase option is normally used for business property, for example, when the use of a particular building is changed for a short time.

Also, used in conjunction with other mortgages, it allows you to sell at a lower than market value and interest rate, receive a substantial amount of cash that can temporarily be used for other purposes, and repurchase the same property later at a predetermined price. In exercising your option to rebuy, you could then sell it at a higher price.

The Bi-Weekly Mortgage.   The bi-weekly mortgage is an opportunity for you to shorten the term of your loan and reduce the interest costs a slight amount each month. It works this way: You pay half the monthly payment on a fixed rate mortgage every two weeks. That is 26 payments a year to make the 13 monthly installments. The results can be dramatic: A 30-year mortgage can often be paid off in little more than 20 years, saving substantial amounts, perhaps thousands of dollars, in interest.

■ *KEY POINT: Doubling monthly payments dramatically lowers interest paid.*

Often slightly lower interest rates are available for bi-weekly loans, since payments must be made twice as often. An automatic payment plan, such as a money market account the bank extracts the payment from directly, is often advisable. For many people who are paid every other week, the bi-weekly mortgage can be a little bit more convenient.

■ *KEY POINT: The interest rate for a bi-weekly mortgage is often less because of the lender's faster recapture of capital.*

In a bi-weekly mortgage, each payment is half of what you would normally give to the bank each month under a conventional mortgage, but you are paying it twice a month. With the exception of February, all months are a few days longer than four weeks, so you actually make 26 payments a year, not 24—an extra month's installment. This can mean a tremendous amount of savings. Take a $100,000 bi-weekly mortgage. At 10%, your payments would be $439 and you would wind up paying $878 more a year than if you paid monthly. However, you would be paying almost $58,000 less in interest, plus you would retire your mortgage in approximately 20 years rather than 30—a substantial saving for those who can organize themselves and who have the extra income to pay the mortgage every other week.

These are only a few of the many ways in which you can finance real estate. They point out that unique arrangements can be made when the motivations of buyers and sellers are strong.

In the following chapters we will discuss more of these techniques. You will see how these techniques can be used to your best advantage and how complex arrangements can be made to gain satisfactory financing in the quickest possible time.

HOME EQUITY LOANS

Home equity loans are a speedy way to raise cash. Instead of refinancing your mortgage or negotiating a second mortgage, consider what is basically a readily accessible line of credit backed up by the equity in your home.

■ *KEY POINT: A home equity loan is a line of credit backed up by the equity in your home.*

As you have seen, mortgage interest is still by and large deductible under the latest tax code, making it one of the only ways in which to borrow money with tax-free interest.

CASH IN YOUR HOME SECURED BY A MORTGAGE

An equity loan or equity credit line is credit secured by a mortgage on your home. Essentially, the unmortgaged value or equity of your home is turned into a revolving line of credit that can be easily tapped by a check or credit card.

A home equity loan is usally priced at a modest two percentage points above the prime rate; therefore it can be thought of as an attractive means of raising extra cash. Conventional second mortgages can often run three to four percentage points higher than first mortgages.

■ *KEY POINT:*   *A home equity loan is an attractive alternative to a higher-priced second mortgage.*

One of the problems with a home equity loan is that the interest rate is not fixed but usually based on the prime rate. This allows it to float upwards and downwards, which can often mean a higher rate in an uncertain future. Further, like a second mortgage, this loan is secured by a lien on your home, and you do run the risk of losing your property if you get in over your head and can't pay. You must approach the home equity loan with caution, but if you need some cash it is one of the options to explore.

■ *CAUTION NOTE:*   *Interest rates can escalate in the future.*

■ *CAUTION NOTE:*   *Use caution, as difficulty in paying can mean the possible loss of your home.*

MAJOR TYPES OF HOME EQUITY LOANS

The first type of home equity loan is one in which the money is borrowed and paid back over a specific period of time with a fixed or floating interest rate.

Essentially, choosing between a fixed or floating interest rate depends on what the rates are when you originate the loan. It is similar to choosing between conventional and adjustable rate mortgages—it may be better to pay the fixed rate, although a little higher, because you know that the interest is not going to change.

Another type of home equity loan is the equity line of credit, in which you may not take the total amount you negotiate for at one time but draw on it as you need it, thereby paying interest only on the amount used. The disadvantage is that you pay the closing charges on setting up the credit line whether you use the money or not. Generally you repay this type of loan in monthly installments that pay interest on the money you've taken and the reduced principal. Interest rates can be either fixed or floating, and although you may wish to negotiate an advantageous fixed rate, most banks only offer this type of loan with a floating rate.

- *CAUTION NOTE:*   *Closing costs are the same regardless of the amount drawn.*

- *KEY POINT:*   *A floating interest rate is the most common in an equity line of credit.*

COMPARING BASIC ELEMENTS

Home equity loans were invented several years ago, and most banks now offer them. Let's look at some of the basic elements of a home equity loan, so that when you talk to various banks about this possibility you can make the following comparisons.

How Will the Rate of Interest Change?

The interest rate for a home equity loan is generally not fixed. In this way it is similiar to the interest rate on an adjustable rate mortgage. Most banks use the prime rate as an index, adding on the average two percentage points to set the beginning rate for the borrower. Usually this rate is adjusted monthly, but some banks adjust it quarterly.

■ *KEY POINT: The prime rate plus two points is a commonly used
index for home equity loan interest.*

The bank will want to set some parameters for the loan. A
particular point for you to be cautious about is the base interest
rate, the minimum rate the bank will want to charge. The problem is that if your rate is set at two percentage points over the
prime rate but the bank has set a 12½% base rate, you could
still be paying 12½% even when the prime rate is 9%.

■ *CAUTION NOTE: A high base rate stops the loan interest from
drifting lower.*

Again, as with adjustable rate mortgages, beware of a low
promotional rate offered to make the loan look like a good deal.
For example, a lender might charge 8% for the first six months
of your loan and then convert to the prime plus two percentage
points. If you want a deal like this, make sure the six-month
period starts when your loan closes and not upon the date of
application.

■ *CAUTION NOTE: A low promotional rate can escalate rapidly.*

Second, you want to make sure that you can afford the
higher payment six months later. If you can barely squeak by
paying the lower, introductory interest rate, you may not be able
to meet the payments when the rate jumps up three or four
points.

■ *CAUTION NOTE: When the rate rises, larger payments can cause
difficulty.*

The variable rate loans usually have some sort of cap on the
interest rate over a set period of years, such as five years or over
the life of the loan. That's not the way most banks want to
negotiate their home equity loans with you. However, compe-

tition among banks is forcing them to come up with some new techniques, such as letting you lock in an interest rate cap at origination or at some future time. They even allow a conversion to a conventional loan, which might be appropriate when you have solved your immediate short-term cash needs.

■ *KEY POINT: Possible conversion to a conventional loan may be allowed.*

How Much Money Can You Borrow?

Generally, as with most conventional loans, mortgage lenders will lend or extend a line of credit up to 70 or 80% of your home's unencumbered equity. Let's understand what this means. If you have a home valued at $200,000 but already have a balance on a first mortgage of $75,000, the bank is not going to lend you 80% of the $200,000 but up to 80% of the remaining equity of $125,000. Your line of credit is thus $100,000.

■ *KEY POINT: The maximum loan is 80% of equity only.*

For homes valued over $250,000 most banks tighten the rules somewhat, allowing perhaps only 75% instead of 80% of unencumbered equity as a line of credit. Again, this is a matter of negotiation and, often, going to the bank that holds your present mortgage to negotiate a home equity loan. If you have a good payment record that assures the bank you will be able to make these higher payments, they will look favorably on your request for the highest credit line possible.

■ *KEY POINT: A consistent record of payments is helpful in securing an equity loan from your current mortgage holder.*

The question of how much money you wish to borrow under the equity line of credit may be based on how much of the amount will be deductible.

How Do Closing Costs Vary?

When you got your first mortgage for your home, whether it was a conventional or an adjustable rate loan, your closing costs probably averaged between 3 and 4% of the amount of money you were borrowing. An equity line of credit also involves some closing costs. Generally they will not be quite as much but approximately ½ or 1–2%, depending on your area.

■ *KEY POINT:* *Closing costs for a home equity loan are usually half of those for first mortgage.*

These closing costs can be extensive, however, and you must remember that you are not borrowing all the money you are signing up for at the time of closing. The loan is a line of credit, and you are going to take it out as you need it, but must pay the closing costs up front based on the whole amount of the credit line. If you are taking out an equity line of credit of $80,000 and your fee is $1,150, that is 1.4% of the loan amount. It sounds reasonable, but if you only use $30,000, the closing cost of $1,150 is 3.8%.

■ *CAUTION NOTE:* *Closing costs are based on the potential amount that can be borrowed.*

In other words, you have paid considerably more in closing costs than you needed to. Closing costs don't make sense unless you are going to receive in the short term the largest portion of the amount of the loan you negotiate.

What is included in the loan fees? Service fee for the bank, legal fees, and a new title insurance policy (this will not always be required if you are negotiating with the same bank). As with your first mortgage, an appraisal, perhaps documentary tax stamps, and recording fees also need to be paid. You can charge these closing costs off as your first draw rather than come up with extra cash.

Schedule of Repayment

Your monthly payment of interest and principal is usually calculated as a percentage of the combined principal and interest outstanding, with the interest repaid first at the end of each billing period. If there is any amount that remains to be paid at the end of this term, it is usually covered with a balloon payment.

You must remember that with an equity credit line loan you are only drawing off money as you need it, so your payments may not be high until you start borrowing a large amount of money. A 1–2% minimum monthly interest rate is common. What you must remember is that 2% over the period of a year is 24%. You want to make sure that you are reducing as much principal as possible, thereby negotiating the lowest possible interest rate.

■ *KEY POINT: A lower amount of initial borrowing is reflected in lower payments.*

Some banks allow repayment of interest on a monthly basis, withholding the payment on any principal until the end of the loan as a balloon payment. This is advantageous. For example, if because of your job or personal requirements you must sell your home, perhaps at the end of five years, you can sell and pay off the amount of money you borrowed through the credit line.

■ *KEY POINT: Paying interest first works well if you will be selling in the near future.*

In either of these cases, should any additional payment of principal be made, banks usually will not charge a penalty. It may be an opportunity for you if you receive an inheritance or other large gain prior to the end of the mortgage term.

DEDUCTIBILITY OF HOME EQUITY LOANS

Since equity line of credit loans were introduced, the rules for interest deductibility have changed. Now all interest on home equity loans up to $100,000 is deductible. This is much simpler than the previous deductibility, which was limited to the amount borrowed up to the purchase price of your home and the costs of any improvements.

■ *KEY POINT: Interest is deductible up to $100,000.*

Previously, only interest on loans for financing, medical treatment, and educational expenses such as tuition and fees for you or your family was deductible. This method was difficult to calculate, as you had to calculate the average unpaid balance of your mortgage for the year in question. So, the new home equity loan rule is a genuine tax boon, allowing you to deduct interest on the loan up to $100,000 ($50,000 if you are married and filing separately).

However, regardless of how the money is used, the loan cannot exceed your house or second home's fair market value. Beyond $100,000, while still borrowed against equity on your home, the amount of interest deducted will depend on the way any excess money is spent. If used in business it is fully deductible, but if used for investment it can be deducted only up to the amount of investment income plus $4,000. If used for another purpose, the money is treated as a consumer loan with minimal deductibility of only 20% in 1989, 10% in 1990, and none after that.

■ *KEY POINT: Interest on home equity funds over $100,000 used in business is fully deductible.*

■ *CAUTION NOTE: Interest on funds over $100,000 used for invest-ment purposes is deductible only to extent of the investment income plus $4,000.*

Who benefits? Under the old rule there was no limit to the deductibility if the money went to educational or medical ex-penses for you or your dependents. Now, with the limit at $100,000, you can do anything with that money without in-fringing upon its deductibility; beyond $100,000 it is deductible only if used for business. If you have several children attending college at the same time and your tuition expenses are high, the home equity loan can benefit you as long as you don't go over the $100,000. You can particularly benefit from getting a home equity loan if you bought your house years ago when real estate prices were low. There is plenty of equity in your property now against which the bank can extend you a line of credit.

■ *CAUTION NOTE: Interest on home equity funds in excess of $100,000 is not deductible even if the loan is for college tuition.*

Note that the money from a home equity loan is not usually used to acquire property or improve a residence. It is more often used to meet outside financial obligations such as college tuition.

Proceeds of the loan are fully deductible as long as the debt does not exceed the lesser of fair market value of your home, minus the existing mortgage balance, or $100,000 ($50,000 if married and filing separate returns). Even if you own two homes as primary and secondary residences, the tax cap on your home equity debt cannot exceed $100,000.

Keep in mind this $100,000 ceiling on a home equity loan. If you are just purchasing your first home and don't need the money right away, maximize the mortgage used to purchase your home. In this way you can save what money you need later on, so that when you want to get your home equity loan you don't eat into your $100,000 equity ceiling.

■ *CAUTION NOTE: The deductible ceiling for the proceeds of a home equity loan is $100,000.*

KEEP BOOKKEEPING IN ORDER

You may benefit by depositing your borrowed money in its own checking account. The Internal Revenue Service has been known to disallow deductions for people who fail to keep track of where their borrowed funds go.

■ *CAUTION NOTE: The IRS may disallow deductions if not backed up by accurate bookkeeping.*

If you keep your home equity loan proceeds in the same account you keep your regular income or investment dividends, it becomes unclear as to how you spent the money. Keep it in a separate account, particularly if the money you are going to be spending is in excess of $100,000. Anything less than $100,000, since it is deductible however you spend it, does not need a special account or even accurate records.

It is not hard to keep track of what is and is not deductible. You will get a monthly statement from your lender showing you the interest that is eligible for a tax deduction if you borrowed under $100,000. If you borrowed more than that, careful records will protect you if you are audited, since you will have to protect anything you deducted beyond the $100,000 from being treated as consumer interest.

■ *KEY POINT: For home equity borrowings beyond $100,000, consider a separate account to keep track of expenses.*

THREE QUESTIONS YOU NEED TO ASK YOURSELF ABOUT APPLYING FOR A HOME EQUITY LOAN

First, is it in your best interest to obtain funds through the equity credit line? Second, is your interest deductibility endangered by the type of investment you make with the money? Third, how constrained are you in spending the money to get the maximum tax benefits?

As with any loan, wise use of the funds is gained without spending cash. The advantage of the credit line is that you do not need to borrow the actual money until you need it. It is essentially a line of credit secured by the equity in your home.

All interest on loans less than $100,000 is deductible no matter how you spend the money. After $100,000 the excess money is deductible only if used in your business or investment up to the amount of your investment income plus $4,000. Otherwise it is regarded as a consumer loan.

■ *KEY POINT:* *Don't draw money or pay interest until it is needed.*

If you manage the funds from a home equity loan carefully, it can be a relatively low-cost way to finance necessary major expenses. The interest rates, although higher than conventional loans, are less than credit card loans of 15 to 20%. And as long as you don't need to borrow more than $100,000, all the interest is deductible.

■ *KEY POINT:* *Interest on home equity loans costs less than that on many other borrowing methods.*

If you borrow more, you can still write off the interest in full if you use the money in your business or if the amount is equal to your investment income plus $4,000.

PROBLEMS WITH BORROWING HOME EQUITY MONEY

A word of caution is in order. Any time you use your existing house as collateral for a loan, you can lose it if you fail to make your payments. In times of fluctuating interest rates, the monthly payment on a home equity loan could rise substantially.

Equally dangerous is a loan that charges interest only, requiring you to pay back the balance of the loan in a single sum at some future time. This would cause you either to sell your home to pay off the loan or take out another loan at a much higher interest rate.

■ *CAUTION NOTE: A potential rise in rate, hence payments, and a balloon payoff can endanger home ownership.*

Banks benefit greatly by lending out their money through a home equity program. Their interest rate, averaging two percentage points over prime, guarantees them a profit no matter how the financial markets may fluctuate. To you these loans can be a real danger if the interest rates climb or if your income declines.

So beware. If rates climb, repayment can drag on for many years. The situation is made more difficult by many banks that advertise a low rate to get you started and in three to six months, convert that rate to a much higher one.

Look for a bank that will give you a cap on the interest rate, and avoid a repayment plan that doesn't allow you to pay off the principal on the loan on a regular basis. Further, a balloon payment coming at the end of the term could create a major financial problem. Even though a bank might allow you an extended period of time to pay, it usually means that less principal is being paid to bring down the loan's balance. Even if the bank allows small payments, it may take years to repay a modest loan.

Again, you should borrow only what you can afford, and you want to make sure that any disclosure problems that might affect the terms of your loan are written in the loan agreement.

Also, if possible, try to negotiate at what time in the future the home equity loan can be converted to a conventional loan. This will be to your advantage if the interest rate on conventional financing drops.

■ *KEY POINT: Negotiate converting your home equity loan to a conventional loan sometime in the future.*

WHY A HOME EQUITY LOAN IS WORTH CONSIDERING

For financing a major expense, such as college tuition or medical bills, the home equity credit line is one way to tap the substantial equity you may have in your home. As with negotiating other loans where the interest rate can fluctuate, it is wise to go with the loan that has an interest rate cap so that you will still be able to afford the payments if the rates rise to that maximum. Further, as with any mortgage borrowing, payments should not exceed one-third of your before-tax income.

■ *KEY POINT: As with any mortgage loan, keep payments within one-third of your budget.*

A home equity loan is an excellent way to borrow without refinancing your first mortgage. It is like a second mortgage, only more flexible. You don't need to take the money until you actually need it, so you don't pay the interest until you put the money to use.

The competition among banks for these loans is extensive, and many banks don't go through the full mortgage process such as appraisal, credit check, and legal fees if they are particularly anxious to give the loan.

■ *KEY POINT: Competition between banks keeps down the cost of services.*

The best possible bank to turn to is the one that already holds your first mortgage. This can be checked when you talk to lenders about waiving many of the closing costs.

■ *KEY POINT: The best bank to approach is the one that holds your present mortgage.*

Banks are very competitive on these types of loans because they benefit from them, and you in turn can benefit by gaining a bank's quick decision on your application. With the proper information you can usually secure a commitment within 24 hours.

■ *KEY POINT: Banks are often motivated to make rapid decisions.*

With the home equity loan you can take the full amount of the money immediately, as you would on a second mortgage, or you can take it as you need it by using a check or, with special arrangements, a credit card. Refinancing and second loans can usually run 5 to 15 years; home equity loans often run longer and can even be open-ended.

This is an excellent way to finance major expenses such as education or medical needs, as long as you are aware of the problems. First, you want to minimize closing costs, as these fees must be paid up front. Second, realize that you have put your house up for security as collateral, which can be a risk if you are unable to make payments. The interest might fluctuate. You don't want the bank to come after your house.

Finally, certain items such as cars are not good to buy with the home equity line of credit, since the pay-back period for a home equity loan is usually longer than that for a car loan. At the end of a few years you could have an unpaid balance for the car of substantially more money than it is worth. A normal car loan is paid off in three or four years, approximating the declining value of the vehicle.

■ *CAUTION NOTE:* **Only finance purchases of significant need or value.**

A home equity loan is one of the major ways you can get at your accumulated equity without selling your house, refinancing it, or taking out a second mortgage. You can simply get a line of credit for the amount of value over your first mortgage that you have in your home. It usually costs less than refinancing and takes less time.

REFINANCING YOUR **12** EXISTING LOAN

In this chapter we consider the refinancing of an existing loan, perhaps with an additional amount of money to be gained.

SAVING MONEY THROUGH REFINANCING

Millions of people who got mortgages between 1986 and the present are benefiting from fairly modest interest rates (at least compared with mortgage rates of the last 15 years). But many who obtained mortgages between 1978 and 1985 are burdened with high rates, often at double digit levels.

If you have a mortgage at one of these higher rates, you have a great opportunity to replace it with one at a lower rate, giving you a chance to save a great deal of money.

■ *KEY POINT: Today's modest rates offer an opportunity to refinance high-interest mortgages.*

When the rates were high, we had no other choice but to negotiate a mortgage at whatever rate was available. The advantage of owning a property far outweighed the few extra points we had to pay for interest. Generally, in addition to a place to live and its attendant tax advantages, ownership meant appreciation, a financial advantage over renting that far outweighed a higher interest rate on a mortgage.

■ *KEY POINT:* *Often the benefits of appreciation, as well as having dwelling space and tax advantages, can outweigh the drawbacks of a high-interest mortgage.*

If the restructured mortgage is simply for the remaining principal balance, running the same number of years but with a lower interest rate will reduce your monthly mortgage payment considerably and save you thousands of dollars in interest over the life of the mortgage.

You may even wish to stretch out the term of your loan as an additional way to keep the mortgage payments down. Or even if you can afford higher monthly payments, you can negotiate your refinancing for a shorter period of time, such as 15 years instead of 25, to get the loan paid off as soon as possible.

■ *KEY POINT:* *Restructuring can gain a lower rate or change the payment term.*

RENEGOTIATING WHEN IT IS TO YOUR ADVANTAGE

Many of you already have financing on your properties, and the terms on which you originated these loans may be very favorable, both in interest rate and monthly payments. However, if you negotiated the loan at a time when interest rates were high, you may very well want to consider what can be done to renegotiate both payments and rate, and even reconsider the amount of time before the loan is paid off. If you don't negotiate the lowest possible deal, you may be paying thousands of extra dollars more than you need to.

■ *CAUTION NOTE: Staying with a high-interest loan is very expensive over time.*

Renegotiating an existing loan is not a difficult process. Usually, if you've had the loan for several years, the principal amount of the loan has diminished and the value of the property has increased, thereby making the proportional share of equity to loan amount very favorable and secure. From the bank's point of view, you are an excellent candidate for a restructured loan, and they may even allow you to borrow some more money if desired.

■ *KEY POINT: Lowered principal balance and higher value are the basis for restructuring.*

Banks don't usually go looking for these loans. Unless a lender can get a higher interest rate, which, obviously, on an existing loan you are not going to agree to, you are not going to be solicited for refinancing. Lenders want to sell new loans at the highest possible rate.

■ *CAUTION NOTE: In times of lower rates banks don't solicit the business of restructuring loans.*

In restructuring a loan, be aware that under the new tax reform laws all of your interest costs may not be deductible. For a thorough explanation of what is deductible see the section on deductibility in the last chapter.

TARGETING THE LEAST EXPENSIVE MONEY

Normally the first mortgage, whether an original loan or a refinancing, is the cheapest money you can borrow. Anything else, commercial loans, a second mortgage, or even a home equity loan, generally costs more in interest rate and has less favorable terms.

■ *KEY POINT:* *First mortgage interest is generally less than that for other types of financing.*

Just as there are many ways to negotiate first mortgage loans, there are many ways to restructure your existing loan. The most common loan is the monthly amortization with constant monthly payments paid over a set time, normally varying anywhere from 15 to 30 years. By negotiating a lower interest rate for this type of loan, you will pay substantially less money out in interest over the long term.

Another way to renegotiate your loan is to keep the same interest rate but, if you are financially able, change the term from 25 or 30 years to 20 or 15 years. The savings can be dramatic, as shown in Figure 12.1.

	30-year loan	20-year loan
Principal amount	$75,000	$75,000
Interest rate	11 percent	11 percent
Number of payments	360	240
Monthly payment	$714	$774
Additional amount	—	$60
Overall interest cost	$182,040	$110,760
Savings	—	$71,280

Figure 12.1. Term comparison.

■ *KEY POINT:* *A lower interest rate or a shorter term can save considerable money.*

As with first mortgages, you can also make more rapid re-payments or make lump-sum reductions of loans, such as balloon payments, at specific periods or at the end of the loan term.

RENEGOTIATING THE BEST TERMS

You should be aware of the basics about any loan you renegotiate. One basic is negotiating to repay that loan in a bulk amount, say from a sale of the property, without incurring any points or penalty. Another is negotiating a minimal amount of penalty should you need to close the loan out before the end of its term.

■ *KEY POINT: In renegotiating an existing loan, you can often eliminate any prepayment penalty.*

As just mentioned, if you are not changing the interest rate but simply the term, usually the bank is quite happy to waive any prepayment penalties.

DISCOUNTING THE LOAN BALANCE

Most people, at the time they sell their property, pay the entire principal balance of their mortgage on that property. Certainly, the lender allows little choice in this matter; full payment is required at the time of the closing, and the bank often handles the paperwork to make sure they get their money.

However, one possibility that you may wish to explore with your bank, although admittedly not one that banks usually favor, is discounting the loan balance. The truth is, lenders faced with low interest rates socked in for a long term might very well be willing to discount the principal balance in order to get back the bulk of their money to lend out at a higher rate.

■ *KEY POINT: Lenders, on occasion, discount the principal balance for a long-term, low-interest loan.*

If the reason you are paying off the loan is the sale of your property, your negotiating position with the lender is nil. But if there is no specific action that would cause a change in your mortgage, you may propose that if the bank will take a discounted payoff in the principal amount due on your loan, they can then reinvest these monies more profitably. Your approach to them might be that you have come into some extra money, perhaps from a family inheritance, and want to pay off the mortgage, but only if discounted.

■ *CAUTION NOTE: If a lender suspects a sale, discounting is not a possibility.*

Usually, if the loan is profitable, the lender is not interested in discounting; banks want to close out only those loans that are unprofitable for them, particularly because of a low interest rate or lack of points.

■ *CAUTION NOTE: Profitable loans cannot be discounted.*

You are not likely to get the lender to agree to a large discount; at most you will get 20 or 30%. The lender must re-lend it at a much better rate than the discounted rate to make money in discounting the payoff to you.

It is helpful in negotiating for you to know the rate of return on alternative investments available to the lender. For example, if you have an old 8% loan and current rates are 13%, the bank may very well be convinced to allow you some discount in order to get most of their investment back.

■ *KEY POINT: Knowing alternative rates will help in negotiating a discount with your lender.*

COSTS OF REFINANCING

You need to be concerned with more than just interest rates. Other factors such as points and prepayment penalties need to be considered in a decision about refinancing. Termite inspection or other wood-boring insect inspection may be required by a lender. These costs can vary between $40 and $60. Often the lender may want to update the credit report, which costs anywhere from $30 to $45. Perhaps an application fee will be charged, although it might be waived when you are refinancing with the lender who currently holds your mortgage. A new appraisal fee is often waived, too, especially if you follow the advice in the first chapter and update much of the information on the property and your own personal financial statements—both crucial to the lender—yourself.

■ *KEY POINT: Numerous loan charges, although often less than those for originating the first mortgage, come with refinancing.*

Points are often the largest obstacle to refinancing. The lender may want to charge one or more percentage points of the mortgage amount in order to make the deal. This amount has to be weighed against what you hope to save.

■ *CAUTION NOTE: Excessive points must be compared with what will be saved.*

Some other charges, such as recording fees, will apply to the new financing. Some banks also require title insurance, the cost of which can vary greatly from bank to bank. The title search is often done by the private attorney you hire, who in turn certifies the title of the property to the bank. This fee may be discounted if you are refinancing your loan with the existing bank. At the very least, the lawyer or whoever you had do the title search in the beginning may give you a discount on doing it again.

Be sure to consult your personal attorney if you refinance, to make sure that there are not any hidden costs and services and that documents are recorded as they should be.

■ *KEY POINT: Always consult your personal attorney.*

Generally, refinancing costs are not as steep as the original costs. Restructuring may sound like a simple transaction of exchanging the balance of your existing mortgage for a new loan carrying a lower interest rate, and with the same lender it is less complicated than the original negotiations. With a new lender, however, the costs may be higher.

Doing business with the lender that carries your existing loan allows them to be more flexible in discounting the costs of refinancing. For example, a credit check probably is not going to be required if you have a good record of paying your present mortgage. Even so, the same bank is likely to charge points, but often not as many on refinancing as on the original loan.

■ *KEY POINT: Doing business with the same lender generally means fewer closing costs.*

MAKING THE DECISION

Many factors will affect your decision on refinancing a property. One is the burdensome cost of an existing first mortgage combined with a second mortgage or even a consumer loan. You may be better off with a new first mortgage that will encompass these other loans, perhaps going back to the original loan amount or even exceeding it. Even if you use this money to pay other things besides your existing loan balance on the property, you might be saving a great deal of interest overall.

■ *KEY POINT: Refinancing can consolidate several loans and add additional monies.*

Usually refinancing is more important if you are going to keep your property for a long time. The extra charges involved in restructuring a loan, although not as great as negotiating the original loan, can bring down your overall savings unless you plan to stay in the property. If you are considering selling in the very near future, it may actually pay you to keep going with your current higher rate.

■ *CAUTION NOTE: Costs to close a loan can be excessive unless you hold the property for several years.*

The primary reason you want to renegotiate a loan is to get a lower interest rate than that on your present mortgage. The danger is that the benefits of refinancing may be offset by its higher expenses. While refinancing may be easy to get, you should shop around among lenders to see what costs are involved and if it is worthwhile for you.

It is difficult to offer a fixed formula for making a refinancing decision, but a good guide to help you decide is called "The 2½% Solution." Specifically, if the interest rate potentially available to you is 2½% less than what you are currently paying, you plan to stay in your home for more than two years, and the refinancing charges don't exceed $3,000, refinancing may make sense for you.

■ *KEY POINT: As a guideline, refinance when the potential interest rate is 2½% less than your current rate.*

The 2½% solution assumes that your mortgage is large enough to make the restructuring advantageous to you. If the interest rate difference is 2% or less, you must look more carefully at the refinancing charges and the amount of money that you are gaining in the refinancing—that is, whether you are just paying off an existing loan to get lower payments, or your payments are staying the same but you are gaining back some money, perhaps to the level of original financing or even more.

It must be of economic benefit for you to gain that extra money, and it is also obvious that if you are going to be selling your house within a year or two, any small gain may not be worth the difference or the effort. As an example, if you have an $80,000, 25-year mortgage at a 12½% fixed rate, your monthly payment is $872. If you refinance the same mortgage at 9¾%, your monthly payment will be $713, or a savings of $159 per month. If your refinancing costs are $3,000, it will take you approximately 19 months to recoup these charges before you begin to see any real savings on your mortgage. If you are staying appreciably longer than two years in your property, then refinancing makes sense.

■ *KEY POINT: Savings are gained once closing costs are recouped.*

A further example: if you presently have a 30-year, $65,000 mortgage with a fixed rate of 13½%, you can refinance with a 20-year loan at 10½%, assuming your refinancing costs are modest and you will be in your home for at least four or five years. This extra 3% difference in interest makes the restructuring worthwhile, because at 13½% you are paying $745 each month, and by refinancing at 10½% you are paying $649, a savings of $96 per month. If your refinancing charges amount to $3,400, it will take you 35 months to save money.

What also must be weighed is the beneficial aspect of paying the loan off in a shorter time. Again, the key is staying in the property beyond the time it takes to pay your refinancing charges.

In another example, assume you have a 25-year, 11½% fixed rate mortgage of $55,000, which you can refinance for 20 years at 10½%. You are presently paying $559 monthly; after refinancing, your monthly costs will be $549, a savings of only $10. Assuming refinancing charges of $3,500, it will take you more years than the mortgage will run to regain this closing money. As in the last example, you are paying off your loan in 20 years under the new refinancing rather than the original 30 years. This may sound beneficial, but you must remember that you can almost always pay a mortgage more rapidly than required. In the previous example the monthly payments were close to $100 lower per month; here they are similar enough so that the decision to restructure must be made on the value of paying off the loan earlier.

■ *KEY POINT: In deciding to refinance, compare monthly savings and any change of term against paying off closing costs.*

If you have taken out an adjustable rate loan, the situation is similar. Let's assume that you have a $75,000, 25-year ARM, in which the interest rate in the beginning was 14% but has now declined to 11% because of a general lowering. Your potential new loan is a fixed rate mortgage at 9¾%. The question is, is it worth it to refinance? You are not going to see a significant difference in monthly payments, and it will take a fairly long time to recover your refinancing charges. However, since at some time in the future interest rates on your adjustable rate mortgage are likely to rise again, boosting your present monthly cost, it might be wise for you to go for the lower fixed rate mortgage to ensure yourself against any future rise.

By way of example, when you originated the loan, your ARM at 14% was $903 monthly. Currently, it is 11% and $735 monthly. Refinancing at the lower conventional rate of 9¾% you will pay $668 monthly, and assuming $3,800 in closing charges, it is going to take almost five years before you realize any real savings. However, for security if rates do rise again, which surely they will (historically they seem to cycle upward), the fixed rate mortgage may be the best financial decision for you.

THE BEST SOURCE FOR YOUR REFINANCING NEEDS

Although you should investigate the interest rates and terms of all local lenders, the best place to start negotiating is the lender of your present mortgage.

As you can judge, one of the biggest obstacles to refinancing is the amount of fees and charges you will have to pay. Jumping down from a 13% to a 10% interest may sound good on paper, but if you have to spend $4,000 just to make it happen, it may not be worth it. Your present banker affords you the best opportunity for negotiating lower charges, both on points and matters of title insurance, credit, and appraisal checks.

Your present lender may charge you some points to originate the refinanced loan, but may forgive any prepayment charges that exist in your present mortgage contract. If you go to a new bank, you are going to have to face prepayment penalty points from your old lender, as well as the originating points charged by your new lender. Bear in mind that if you are charged more than three points, refinancing may not be profitable for you.

Your present lender knows that you are serious about paying off your old mortgage; you are bound to gain a most advantageous refinancing deal, perhaps requiring only a point or two instead of the more average three to four points.

■ *KEY POINT:* **Start refinancing negotiations with your present lender.**

Even if your bank sold your mortgage in the secondary market, they continue to service it by collecting the payments, earning an annual servicing fee of approximately ¼–½ of 1% of the total amount of the loan. If you refinance elsewhere, you will be paying off this loan and the original lender will lose this fee, so this lender is most likely to offer you a competitive deal to keep your business.

USING A SECOND MORTGAGE TO RESTRUCTURE YOUR EXISTING FINANCING

Second mortgage loans are always something you should consider in restructuring the financing of your home. There are, however, several attendant dangers. One is that interest rates on a second mortgage are usually not favorable—often they are some of the highest rates consumers can pay. Second, they can add a great deal to the amount of your monthly payments. Not only do you have your existing first loan payments, but you have a second mortgage payment that is secured by your house.

■ *CAUTION NOTE: Rates and overall monthly payments on second mortgages are higher than those on other forms of financial restructuring.*

Just as with home equity credit lines, banks are always anxious to lend money in the form of a secondary mortgage; so, it is easy to negotiate with them in less than a day's time.

Unfortunately, with a second mortgage, the bank often isn't concerned about your assets and balance sheet or verifying your income. Rarely will they even run a credit check. What they are concerned about is the amount of equity or the difference between the value of your property and the principal balance on your first mortgage loan. In a sense, they are making the loan on the basis of your equity rather than on your ability to pay. It can be difficult for those on fixed incomes or those who have many debts, or those whose income may vary because of the nature of their work. Foreclosure is an ever-present risk in negotiating any second mortgage, which makes it a much higher risk than renegotiating your existing first loan.

■ *CAUTION NOTE: Be cautious when you are the only judge of your ability to pay.*

Sometimes negotiating the mortgage can be speedily done, but this is not necessarily the best thing for you. You should always make sure you have a wise use for this money, and that your payments and interest rate are not exorbitant or more than you can comfortably handle.

Many borrowers who have become overburdened and find it difficult to make payments discover that the banks with which they originally negotiated their loans no longer hold them. Their loans have been sold along with other loans to groups of investors, who invariably make the decision to foreclose when payments aren't being made. This sort of abuse can lead to much fraud in the lending industry.

The key thing in getting a second mortgage is making sure there are no terms in the fine print you do not understand and that haven't been negotiated, and that you can meet all your expenses. You must decide if this is better than negotiating additional funds through restructuring your first mortgage loan.

■ *KEY POINT:* *Restructure your first mortgage before considering a second mortgage.*

INTEREST DEDUCTIBILITY IN REFINANCING

Deductibility of mortgage interest in refinancing can fall into two categories: acquisition debt and home equity debt. Acquisition debt is incurred by refinancing your old mortgage up to the amount of the refinanced debt; home equity debt is money generally not used to purchase or improve your property. Your single refinancing, then, can be both acquisition debt and home equity debt.

For example, if you gain more money refinancing your present mortgage balance by using part of the refinancing proceeds to pay off your original mortgage and the rest to pay off a personal debt, even though this is all one loan, it qualifies partially as acquisition indebtedness and partially as home equity indebtedness. The interest on the home equity portion of the new refinanced loan is fully deductible so long as the debt does not equal the lesser of the fair market value of your home minus the total acquisition debt, or $100,000 ($50,000 if you're married and file separate returns). Even if you own two homes, the upper limit on your home equity debt, whether on one or both homes, still may not exceed $100,000.

■ *KEY POINT:* *Interest on refinancing is deductible up to $100,000.*

A note of caution, if you qualify for the new alternative minimum tax (AMT), which is a flat tax rate of 21% for those whose legitimate deductions reduce the regular tax they owe substantially below the amount their income suggests. There are limits on the deductibility of a refinanced mortgage for AMT purposes. A quick way to determine what is deductible under AMT is to divide your old mortgage balance by the total amount of your new loan. The result is the percent of interest on your refinanced mortgage you may deduct.

FOUR-POINT GUIDELINE FOR REFINANCING

First, lock in a favorable interest rate. Do what you can even if it means paying a point or two extra to negotiate the lowest interest rate.

Second, make sure you only refinance for as much money as you absolutely need. Refinancing your property, as we have seen in the discussion on home equity loans, can be an excellent way to gain money for your child's college tuition or for some essential remodeling. It is not the way to buy a car or a boat or any other large depreciable item, or to take an expensive vacation. You are pledging your home as security for the loan, so negotiate the lowest possible charges. Sometimes the interest rate difference can be very attractive, but if the charges and fees to get this loan are too high, it can take you years to reach any true savings on refinancing.

Third, avoid prepayment penalties if possible. If you need to sell in the near future or at any time while your loan is still in existence, you shouldn't be charged for paying your loan before the end of its term. If you cannot avoid a prepayment penalty, make sure that it is a percentage based on the future balance of the loan, not on the original amount.

Fourth, don't refinance if you plan to move within two and a half to three years. The charges needed to make this loan often destroy any savings, unless you plan to remain with the loan, hence the property, for a four- or five-year period. So make sure in refinancing that you're going to be staying put for a while.

MORTGAGES KEEP 13 YOUR TAXES DOWN

In this chapter, we discuss the tax advantages of mortgages and how the current tax law affects the ownership of real estate. Enormous changes have occurred for investors in recent years. The government has done away with tax shelters, and real estate is better for it. Let's see why.

■ *KEY POINT: Owners are better off now that the tax law has eliminated excessive tax shelter benefits.*

One of the major sections of the old tax rule allowed for the excess of mortgage, operating expenses, and "bookkeeping" deductions to overlap onto personal income, which is why, in fact, many high-income types such as doctors and lawyers invested in real estate. The real estate market became clogged with those who wanted to own real estate only for its tax advantages—it became a way for them to pay fewer taxes on huge incomes and to convert their profits from ordinary income to long-term capital gains. They didn't care if the property made money because it sheltered part of their income. Sounds great? Not really, for two reasons. First, it brought people into the real estate market who were more concerned about sheltering their income than about their property. Second, since lower taxes took priority over the price of the property, they contributed to inflated values.

■ *CAUTION NOTE: The provision to shelter income made for bad owners and inflated values.*

The new tax law limits tax deductions to the property itself; no longer can the rich overlay a property's deductions onto their regular incomes. What does this mean? Simple. It puts the value of income property back where it belongs: on income! The new tax law, in limiting tax deductions, rewards the income property produces.

However, an important exception allows many taxpayers to offset their employment income with rental losses. If your adjusted gross income is less than $100,000, you may take up to $25,000 in losses on rental property that you actively manage. To be "active" you must own a minimum of 10% of the property and make decisions on maintenance, rents, and tenant selection. You can also hire a manager and be considered active provided you can verify your guidance in these decisions. If you make between $100,000 and $150,000, for every $1 in income over $100,000, you lose 50 cents of allowable losses. For example, if you earn $125,000, you can only deduct $12,500.

If you are rich and make more than $150,000, no losses can shelter regular income. If you are in this category, don't worry, however. This tax rule only involves tax reporting, not cash flow. You have only lost a tax shelter, and as long as your rental income covers mortgage payments and operating expenses, what losses you incur on paper can be accumulated and eventually applied against any profits when you sell, which will boost your return considerably. That is one of the many ways to benefit, as you will see in this chapter.

■ *KEY POINT: The new tax law puts the value of investment property on income.*

TAX BREAKS IN REAL ESTATE FINANCING

The traditional tax break, retained under the current law, is the deductibility of mortgage interest. As we have seen, the interest payment is the largest part of the total mortgage payment, especially in the first few years. Under the current tax law, this deductibility, with exceptions, is generally kept for up to two homes. The deduction also remains on property owned for business or investment.

Current rules apply to any loans secured by the main home, including first and second mortgages. Whether your home mortgage interest is deductible depends on the date you took out the mortgage, the amount of the mortgage, and use of its proceeds. On mortgages originated after October 13, 1987, for interest to be fully deductible, the amount of debt to acquire the home may not exceed $1 million. Interest on any first $100,000 of home equity indebtedness is also fully deductible. More on this in the next section.

■ *KEY POINT: Mortgage interest is still deductible on up to two homes and on all investment property.*

Another benefit under the new tax law is the full deductibility of property taxes assessed against your home, including a second home or investment property. In fact, the deductions of mortgage interest and property taxes are the two greatest encouragements to buy real estate the government could give us.

Another benefit goes beyond the deductibility of interest and taxes. For income or business property you can deduct operating expenses: lawn care, maintenance, heating fuel, electricity, telephone, management services, trash removal, and so forth. For example, if you live in one-half of a duplex and rent out the other side, any expenses related to the operation of the rented

Tax Rates. Currently, there are three effective tax rates: 15% for joint filers with income under $29,750; 28% above that figure up to $71,900; and 33% up to $149,250, then dropping back down to 28%. For single filers the breakpoints are $17,850 for 28%; $43,150 for 33%; and $89,560 for the return to 28%. Married filing separately; 15% under $14,875 and then 28% up to $35,950; 33% to $113,300; and 28% thereafter. Head of household is $23,900 for 28%; $61,650 for 33%; and $123,790 for the return to 28%. Note that the third level of tax, 33%, is the result of the imposition of a 5% additional tax that eliminates the benefit of personal exemptions for those with higher levels of income, after which the 28% marginal tax bracket is, in essence, restored.

Standard Deduction. The standard deduction for single taxpayers is $3,000; for married people filing jointly, $5,000; for heads of household, $4,400; and for married filing separately, $2,500. These deductions will be adjusted for inflation.

Personal Exemption. The base exemption is $2,000, but it will be adjusted for inflation. The law effectively eliminates the benefit of the exemption for high-income taxpayers. If income rises above the following levels of adjusted gross income, a surtax of 5% is added: $89,560 for single individuals; $149,250 for joint filers; $123,790 for heads of households; and $113,300 for marrieds filing separately. The surtax starts at these levels and remains until it recaptures all the tax saving gained by claiming exemptions.

Mortgage Interest. In most cases, mortgage interest is deductible only for first and second homes. Specifically, on mortgages originating after October 13, 1987, the interest is fully deductible only if the amount of acquisition indebtedness does not exceed $1 million. Interest on the first $100,000 of home equity indebtedness is fully deductible.

Other Interest. The interest on car loans, credit cards, personal loans, and other consumer debt (other than home mortgages) is 10% in 1990, and not deductible at all thereafter. Interest on borrowings to finance investments is deductible only to the extent of investment income.

State and Local Taxes. The itemized deduction for state and local income and property taxes is fully deductible. There are, however, no deductions for sales taxes.

Capital Gains. Preferential tax treatment for long-term capital gains for real estate and other assets does not at present exist. Even though the capital gains language is in the current tax code, capital gains are taxed just like wages at ordinary rates up to 33%. Under the old law, pre-1987, 60% of a capital gain was excluded from tax, making a top rate of 20% for assets held longer than six months.

(Continued)

Figure 13.1. Highlights of the current tax law.

Tax Shelter Losses. Taxpayers are no longer able to use investment real estate losses to offset employment income. An exception is allowed for landlords who actively manage their own properties, who can use up to $25,000 in losses to offset their other income. This benefit is phased out for those with adjusted gross incomes between $100,000 and $150,000. Another exception allows investors in low-income and real estate rehabilitation projects up to $25,000 in losses, with the phase-out range being upped to between $200,000 and $250,000.

Property Depreciation. Under the current law properties used for business or investment must be depreciated over 27½ years for residential and 31½ for commercial. The code contains no provision for accelerated depreciation.

Home Transfer. Homesellers don't have to pay taxes on a gain from selling a home as long as they plow it into another home within 24 months.

One-Time Exclusion. In the current law, there is the one-time $125,000 exemption from taxes on home-sale profits for people 55 years of age and over. These homeowners must have owned and lived in their main home for at least three years out of the five-year period ending on the date of the sale or exchange, and neither spouse can have excluded gain on the sale of a home since July 26, 1978.

Figure 13.1. (*Continued*)

side are deductible. For the half you live in, as in a single-family residence, only mortgage interest and property taxes can be deducted from your taxable income. You can even rent out a room and deduct the portion of operating expenses that relate to the room that is rented out.

■ *KEY POINT: Property tax is still deductible.*

■ *CAUTION NOTE: Operating expenses, beyond mortgage interest and property taxes, are not deductible for a residence.*

■ *KEY POINT: The operating expenses for income or commercial property are deductible.*

In fact, as we've just seen, if your income is under $100,000, any excess deductions on investment property can shelter up to $25,000 of regular income.

A further tax benefit lies in the use of a home office. You can make a percentage deduction of operating expenses for the part of your home you use for business or investment purposes. To do this, figure the square feet of space you use for business as a percentage of the total square footage of your house, or, if the rooms are approximately the same size, figure what percentage the rooms used for business are of the total number of rooms. Then apply that percentage to the total of each home operating expense. For example, if you use one room of your five-room house as an office, you can deduct twenty percent of your heat, telephone, yard-care, and other property expenses.

Normally home-use expenses for yard care and landscaping are not deductible, though you can deduct a part of the cost of painting the outside of your home or repairing the roof.

Note that there are strict qualifications in deducting for home office use. To qualify, an area of your home must be used exclusively for the home office at all times. Any exception disqualifies the deduction. In addition, the home office must be a condition of employment (for employees), or you must be self-employed and working from your home. Also, if you are self-employed the IRS requires you to disclose that you are claiming deductions for a home office—a red flag for audits.

■ *KEY POINT: A home office provides a tax deduction.*

A major tax break is the deferral of tax when you sell your home. Earlier we discussed how taxes cannot be deferred in the sale of investment property unless there is a bona fide exchange with another investor. But when you sell a private residence, you can defer the tax up to two years by buying property of the same or higher value, into which the tax basis of your old home is transferred. You defer the tax by exchanging one house for another. This is similar to investment property, except the exchange must be ongoing and completed within six months.

Also, the deferral of profits does not apply to that portion of your home that is used as a home office. You might want to forgo the home office deduction for this reason alone. Specifically, the deductions for depreciation and maintenance are minimal compared to the loss of tax deferral.

■ *KEY POINT: Taxes on the profit gained in selling a private residence are deferred if a new residence is bought within two years.*

■ *KEY POINT: To defer taxable gain on investment property, the exchange must be ongoing.*

■ *CAUTION NOTE: The total deferral of taxable gain can occur only when you acquire property of the same or higher value.*

If you are 55 or older, you have an additional tax benefit when you sell your home. Up to $125,000 of profit is exempt from taxes. Like most of us, you will probably buy and sell your homes, continually trading up to better ones. When you are over 55 and close to retirement, you can sell knowing you are protected by this $125,000 tax savings. If you have a tax-deferred gain on a former house (or houses), you can still keep postponing those taxes on the entire profit until you sell your final home.

■ *KEY POINT: Once you are 55 years old, you benefit by a $125,000 exclusion on the sale of your home.*

After deducting the first $125,000, the tax on the remaining amount is just deferred, not eliminated. Once you sell your last home and become a renter, the deferral ends. You will be obligated to pay the taxes due on the gain from the sale of your last home, plus any deferred gain from sales of your previous homes. However, if you buy or start building a house before your two-year grace period ends, you keep the deferral going.

■ *KEY POINT: A good tax strategy is to keep trading up homes until you are at least 55 years old.*

When you do finally sell your last home or investment, how is the taxable gain handled? What do you pay in taxes? Under the current law the benefit is still substantial. Capital gains are taxed at the same rate as other income. Before 1987, the maximum tax on capital gains was 20%. In effect, that rate now can be 33%, the highest tax bracket of the new system. Note that in the near future, through presidential and congressional action, capital gains may regain their former preferential treatment.

■ *CAUTION NOTE: Capital gains are now taxed as regular income, up to a maximum of 33%.*

Since in the year of sale your taxable income is likely higher than normal, your overall marginal tax bracket will probably be 33%. The difference between 20% and 33%, or 13%, then, is not an unreasonable jump when you consider that under the old law taxes on regular income reached 70%.

■ *CAUTION NOTE: Since a property sale will mean additional income, your taxable income will stretch to the highest bracket of 33%.*

■ *KEY POINT: The difference between 20% and 33% is not significant, considering that before 1987 regular income was taxed up to 70%.*

The tax brackets under the current law are a financial benefit. Now there are three primary rates, 15%, 28%, and 33%, to compute how much the government is owed. The income separating these three brackets varies with your status. If you are married and file jointly with your spouse, you will pay 15% on the first $29,750 in taxable income and 28% up to $71,900, after you have adjusted for exemptions and deductions. Amounts over 28% will be taxed at 33%. The breakpoint for singles is $17,850 for 28% and $43,560 for 33%. However, the benefit of personal exemptions is effectively phased out for upper-income taxpayers, as joint filers starting with a taxable income above $149,250 ($89,560 for single filers) will pay an extra 5% surtax that applies until all the tax savings of the personal exemption are gone. Further, these levels will be adjusted for inflation beginning in 1990.

■ *CAUTION NOTE: Personal exemptions are eliminated for certain high-income taxpayers.*

Another tax-saving opportunity at the time of a property sale is the installment sale. In an installment sale you defer your taxable gain by spreading the payments from a buyer over a period of time. You don't pay the tax on your profit until the year in which you receive it. This means you can sell now and spread out the tax bite on your profit over the years in which you report these installment payments. You might choose to defer them until you retire, when, with a lower income, you may be in the 15% marginal tax bracket. Later in this chapter we will see more on installment sales.

■ *KEY POINT: An installment sale allows a spreading out of payments and thus tax liability.*

■ *KEY POINT: Defer gains until retirement, when lessened income brings you into the 15% tax bracket.*

Another tax benefit of ownership is rental of a second or vacation home. You can receive a write-off on the ownership of a second or vacation home, but the restrictions are more severe than on your primary home. How much you can write off depends on the number of days you rent out your house and how many days you set aside for personal use. If you rent out your vacation home for less than 15 days during the year, you can deduct mortgage interest and property taxes but not maintenance and depreciation.

■ *CAUTION NOTE: Write-offs are still available for second or vacation homes, but follow complex rules.*

If you rent the vacation home for 15 days or more, or more than 10% of the actual use days, whichever is longer, all costs associated with renting are deductible. If you rent for fifteen days or more during the year and use it more than an additional fifteen days, or more than 10% of the number of days it was actually rented, whichever is longer, the deductibility of expenses is based on the percentage ratio between the number of days it is rented and the number of days it is occupied by you.

In some cases, perhaps if you and your spouse's combined income is over $150,000, you may benefit by reclassifying your rental property as a second or vacation home. For example, if you use it yourself for 15 days, or 10% of the number of days you rent it out, whichever is greater, then it qualifies and you can deduct the mortgage interest from your regular income. Note that you would not normally be able to do this if you made over $150,000 and the property was classified as an investment.

Another tax advantage can be contracting your own work. More and more home and property owners are discovering they can benefit by doing some of their capital improvement and maintenance work themselves. For example, if it costs you $30 an hour for a plumber plus a half hour's travel time, to replace a 25-cent faucet packing, you quickly learn how to do it yourself.

Besides saving money, what is the tax benefit? In your own home, a maintenance cost is not deductible, but you can escape the tax on the difference between the cost of an expensive outsider and your own cost in doing the work. Here is how it works. For simplicity's sake, let's assume you pay 40% in combined federal and state taxes. You wish to paint the inside of your house. A contractor wants to charge you $700 for labor and $300 for paint. You have estimated it will cost you only $400 to do the job yourself. To cover the expense of hiring an outsider you will need a before-tax income of $1,667, which, after being discounted the 40% for taxes, is $1,000 to pay the contractor. This is opposed to needing an income of only $667 to pay yourself

$400. A saving of $1,000! Don't pay hard-earned, after-tax dollars to others for a job you can do yourself.

■ *KEY POINT: There is a considerable tax saving in doing your own repair.*

This has only been a sampling of the major tax advantages available in real estate. Now we will more closely examine those that affect real estate financing.

DEDUCTING INTEREST SAVES TAXES

Next to escalating growth, the most popular reason for owning property is the deductibility of interest. Let's see how it works. If on your home you have a $70,000 mortgage at 12¾% interest, payable monthly over a term of 25 years, your monthly payment is $776.34, which adds up to $9,316 per year.

How much of that is interest? At 12¾% the first year's interest is just over $8,900, or $740 per month. As we learned earlier, not much principal is paid in the first year, but in terms of taxes, this is a great benefit. Out of the $9,316 you pay, over $8,900 is deductible. Although you still have to spend the $8,900, you do it with after-tax dollars.

■ *KEY POINT: In the early years of a mortgage, most of the payment is deductible.*

When owning is compared with renting, where the payments cannot be deducted, the difference is pronounced. A renter in the combined 40% federal and state bracket, paying the same $8,900 as rent, needs a before-tax income of $14,833 to afford it. The only amount that you the owner are paying in after-tax income is the $400 that goes toward principal. You can see how interest deductibility promotes home ownership and takes the curse off high interest rates.

■ *KEY POINT: All things being equal, interest deductibility makes renting less advantageous than buying.*

Another advantage is that the interest deduction may reduce your tax bite from the higher 33% to the lower 28%, perhaps even from 28% to 15%, particularly during a time of low employment income.

■ *KEY POINT: A large interest deduction may bring you into a lower tax bracket.*

Note that for deductions to bring a taxpayer's overall rate down to 15%, taxable income after personal exemptions must remain under $17,850 for a single and under $29,750 for a couple. For 28%, income after exemptions must be under $43,150 for singles and $71,900 for joint filers. Even if you pay at the higher rate of 33%, it is only based on the incremental amount above what is allowed in the 28% bracket. Higher income tax couples with joint gross incomes above $149,250, and single taxpayers with more than $89,560, would have to pay at the 33% rate on all their taxable income. Even so, when tax time rolls around each year, knowing that interest payments on mortgage are fully deductible provides some relief.

■ *KEY POINT: Couples filing joint returns can make more before going into the higher 33% bracket.*

DEPRECIATION CUTS
TAXABLE INCOME

Depreciation is a bookkeeping deduction of the "wasting away" of a tangible asset. With real property, you are allowed to depreciate the physical structure, or improvement portion, of your property over a period of time. In an investment or business property, you are allowed to deduct a certain amount over a long-term period. This is accomplished by what is known as straight line depreciation.

■ *KEY POINT: "Bookkeeping" depreciation allows you to deduct for the "wasting away" of the structural portion of a property.*

Depreciation works in the following manner. You own an investment property purchased for $230,000; $40,000 of your purchase price is attributed to the value of the land and $190,000 is the value of the improvement—the apartment or commercial building itself. In a technical sense (although not an actual one unless you forgo maintenance), the property wastes away. You are therefore permitted to depreciate the building portion of your asset over a period of years (a 27½-year schedule for residences and a 31½-year schedule for commercial properties). As an example, we will depreciate the $190,000 building over a period of 27½ years; for accounting purposes we say that 3.64% of the building wastes away each year until everything is gone when that period is over.

It doesn't really waste away, or in most cases even lose value. Over that period of time maintenance and capital improvements will have been made, keeping the building in operable condition.

■ *KEY POINT: Properties don't really "waste away" unless you neglect them.*

However, you benefit by taking this depreciation. In fact, you are required to take it. In the previous example, 3.64% of the $190,000, or $6,916 is deductible, just like your interest or property tax expense, against your rental income. And as we've seen, this amount is deductible up to $25,000 against employment income for those who earn under $100,000 and actively manage.

> ■ *KEY POINT: Investment property owners are required to take depreciation deductions.*

Each year take another 3.64% or $6,916, as a deduction, until the end of 27½ years, when, at least in a bookkeeping sense, your asset wasted away.

KEEPING TRACK OF YOUR TAX BASIS

Depreciation brings up another tax concept, the tax basis. At the time of sale, how do you merge your profit? We will use the example in the last section to show you. If you sell the $230,000 property for the same price three years after purchase, will you have any profit? Of course, since you have reduced its value by the $6,916 deduction taken each year, and three years of depreciation equals $20,748. You now have, for bookkeeping purposes, $169,252 left. To this you add the land's value of $40,000—land does not depreciate—and arrive at $209,252, your new depreciated value and tax basis. So when you sell at the end of three years for $230,000, your profit is $20,748 ($230,000 minus $209,252), the same amount of your depreciation. Are you disadvantaged by selling at the same price? Absolutely not. You have had the full deduction of the $20,748 over the three years, and you only have to pay it back at your ordinary tax rate. For example, if you are in the 28% bracket you have converted a straight deduction of $20,748 into a cost to you of $5,809 ($20,748 times the personal tax rate of 28%)—a bargain!

> ■ *KEY POINT: Your tax basis is your purchase price minus depreciation taken (investment property only), plus any capital improvements.*

Further, if your property's value rises 4% per year, as you might expect, your selling price will be $258,718. Then your taxable profit will be $49,466 ($258,718 minus $209,252). Now you've made more money, again at rates not much more than pre-1987 capital gains rates.

■ *KEY POINT:* *The tax basis allows you to measure your taxable gain upon a sale or exchange.*

You can't depreciate the house you live in unless you rent it out. The purchase price is your tax basis. If you sell a house for $150,000, having bought it for $100,000 five years before, you have a gain of $50,000. If you don't buy again and are under 55 years of age, you add this gain to your regular income, paying tax at the applicable rate.

■ *CAUTION NOTE:* *You are not allowed to depreciate your residence.*

If you buy another house within two years, this tax basis travels with you, being adjusted by the higher or lower price of your new home and any improvements you might make. The gain is calculated in the same way as is an investment property, except that the tax can be deferred until the sale of your final house.

■ *KEY POINT:* *Your tax basis travels with you into the purchase of a new home or into a new investment property upon an exchange.*

As you can see, the major difference between owning a house and owning an investment property, in terms of taxes, is the depreciation deduction. In an investment property, you can deduct depreciation against rental income under a specified schedule on a yearly basis. This, along with your mortgage interest and operating expenses, further reduces the taxes on your annual income.

■ *KEY POINT:* *The difference between a residence and an investment property is the ability to depreciate the improvement portion of the investment property.*

The other difference is that the tax basis for homes does not change, except for major improvements or additions or when transferred to a new property of different value. Your basis in an investment property is reduced by a depreciated amount each year.

■ *KEY POINT:*   *The tax basis for a home does not go down and will go up when capital expenditures are made.*

However, the deduction of depreciation, combined with the deductibility of mortgage interest, property taxes, and other operating expenses, can in many cases offset the income received over the course of the year from the property itself. In some cases this enables you to pocket the money while deferring the actual tax on it.

■ *KEY POINT:*   *The three basic deductions—mortgage interest, property taxes, and depreciation—make income property a superior investment.*

WHEN TO NEGOTIATE A TAX-DEFERRED EXCHANGE

We have shown that you have two years in which to exchange one residence for another, and you can defer your tax if the new house is of the same or higher value than the one sold. The trick, then, is to own a house or keep exchanging houses until you are 55, when you can take advantage of the $125,000 exclusion. You can also defer taxes on the exchange of investment property, but this must be done under strict rules or after a sale you may find you must settle up with the government on the taxable gain of your profit.

■ *KEY POINT:*   *If you follow firm rules, you can defer taxable gains when you exchange one property for another.*

If you exchange an investment property, you can defer the tax in much the same way you can with a house you sell. If you trade up for a property of more value, perhaps putting in some extra cash yourself or agreeing to pay another mortgage, you can escape the entire tax during the year in which you make the trade and defer it until you sell the new property. Like the tax on a house sale and repurchase, the tax on the gain is postponed until you sell the property for a price exceeding its tax basis.

■ *CAUTION NOTE:* *Taxes, when deferred legally through a property transfer, must be paid at the time you sell the last property.*

An exchange is particularly advantageous if you have a large gain from taking accelerated depreciation for a number of years (where the accelerated portion must be recaptured at ordinary income tax rates) or if the depreciable basis of a building has been substantially written off.

■ *KEY POINT:* *An exchange is ideal when you have a low tax basis because of having taken accelerated depreciation, which must be recaptured as ordinary income.*

Exchanging the property will even give you larger tax deductions. It is equivalent to receiving an interest-free government loan on the taxes you would have owed had you sold the property. You keep your capital intact, undepleted by any tax, and can reinvest it with the full value of your old property in a new property.

■ *KEY POINT:* *Deferring tax on a sale is like getting an interest-free government loan.*

Exchanging does have its intricacies. There are real estate people who specialize in them, and their advice on a particular deal can be invaluable. Simply stated, if you exchange one investment, or income-producing, property for another, you qualify for what the IRS calls the "like-kind" exchange, that is, a tax-free exchange. You can exchange a building and land for just land, or a parcel of land for a building with a fast-food tenant. The "like-kind" exchange is restricted to property held for business or investment purposes, so you cannot exchange your residence for a rental property. Also, the trade must occur within 180 days of the signing of the original exchange papers.

■ *CAUTION NOTE:* *The exchange of "like-kind" investment property is subject to specific rules.*

Note that a "dealer," someone who continually buys and sells property, cannot qualify for a tax-free exchange. You can only qualify if you buy and sell on an occasional basis, and only if the property is a long-term investment. Thus the exchange cannot be tax-free if the newly acquired property is offered immediately for resale.

■ *CAUTION NOTE:* *A dealer who buys and sells property cannot defer tax by exchanging property.*

Not all property exchanges are completely tax-free. If the sale includes such things as cash or other property, the gain is taxed up to the amount of this additional cash or property.

■ *CAUTION NOTE:* *Often some tax is paid on a tax-deferred exchange because cash or additional property has been thrown in to balance equity.*

An existing mortgage on an exchange property is treated as extra cash. This is true whether the mortgage is assumed or taken subject to an existing mortgage by the second party. Therefore, if you trade a property worth $100,000 on which there is a $20,000 mortgage for an unmortgaged lot and building worth $80,000, a $10,000 automobile, and $10,000 in cash, you will be receiving $40,000 in extra property—the release of the $20,000 mortgage plus another $20,000 representing the value of the car and cash.

■ *CAUTION NOTE: In an exchange, if you receive full value for a property with an existing mortgage, the difference may be taxed.*

Part or all of this extra property may be taxed to you, depending on whether you realize a gain on the exchange. When you give anything extra, such as cash, equipment, or other property, or assume or take subject to an existing mortgage, you get no loss deduction. It is simply added to your investment, thereby increasing your basis in the new property.

■ *KEY POINT: In an exchange, other property, that is, cash or assumed mortgages, increases your tax basis in the new property.*

If both properties are mortgaged, the party giving up the larger mortgage and obtaining the smaller mortgage treats this difference, or excess, as additional property.

■ *CAUTION NOTE: The difference between mortgages in an exchange is treated as additional property.*

The tax-deferred exchange of either a house or an investment property, despite the intricate rules for each, is a decided advantage of owning real estate. Having a sizeable mortgage can actually make some exchanges easier, because you need less equity in your present property to trade for a highly mortgaged property. This can be a particular advantage if you have difficulty financing a small property. Exchange is a way to trade your equity for a larger property, without the addition of cash, while deferring the tax.

■ *KEY POINT: In an exchange, present equity serves as a down payment on a larger property.*

THE INSTALLMENT SALE TAX BREAK

If you sell a property and don't qualify for the excluson or tax-deferred exchange, you can either report the entire gain in the year of sale or defer part of it on the installment basis. As we saw in the first part of this chapter, this tax-saving opportunity allows you to spread the tax on your profit over the years in which you receive the installment payments.

■ *KEY POINT: Installment sale reporting allows you to spread out your tax over the period in which you receive payments.*

Let's say you make a profit of $95,000 on a home you sell for $125,000. Even when calculated at the current rates, the $31,350 tax ($95,000 × 33%) is a whopping amount to pay. However, instead of paying the entire $31,350 tax in the year you sell, if you take a down payment of $25,000 the first year, then $10,000 plus interest over each of the next 10 years, you only report one-tenth, or $3,135, in each of the 10 years.

Whether buying or selling, if you are planning on an installment sale, consult an accountant or tax attorney.

■ *CAUTION NOTE: Always consult a tax advisor on an installment sale.*

PYRAMIDING YOUR WEALTH WITHOUT PAYING TAXES

As you have seen, mortgage interest and property tax deductions are big benefits. Operating costs are further deductions for the investment property owner. These are not available to renters or those who put their money in investments such as stocks and bonds or precious metals that impose strict rules and borrowing limits on the amount that can be financed. Real estate, in contrast to other investments, can be financed almost completely.

■ *KEY POINT: Even under the current tax law, only by owning real estate can you benefit from financing and tax provisions.*

You can profit from the income from investment property and at the same time build a substantial amount of equity. And when you sell to reclaim your equity, you can pay the tax on the profit at modest overall rates (compared with the pre-1987 rates). Under the current tax law, even though the 20% maximum on capital gains tax has been eliminated, the highest bracket you can be taxed on now is 33%. This is not much of a loss.

And, in fact, you don't always need to pay a tax at the time you sell. If you sell your home because you need larger quarters or need to move away, you have up to two years before you buy or build another one to defer your taxable gain completely, as long as you buy a property of more value. This is also true with investment property, but the rules are more stringent. You must engage in a true exchange with the owner of the second property. Sometimes handled by real estate brokers who specialize in exchanging, this can often involve three or more owners of different properties, all participating in a circular exchange.

■ *KEY POINT: Deferring taxes through exchanges allows you to pyramid your wealth.*

These techniques do not eliminate taxes. The taxes are simply deferred to a future time when you no longer wish to own property. At age 55 or over, when you finally sell, having deferred taxes on perhaps a series of residences, you can exclude $125,000 from your taxable profit. This exclusion doesn't apply to investment property; here, however, the amount you have deferred over the years is now paid with cheaper, inflated dollars.

■ *KEY POINT:*   *Upon selling your last investment property, you pay deferred taxes with cheaper dollars.*

This last, extra benefit is a good reason in itself to defer your taxes.

CHOOSING A KNOWLEDGEABLE ACCOUNTANT

The tax techniques we have discussed here should only be used in consultation with a competent tax advisor. A tax-deferred exchange on investment property is a complex undertaking. To get the most benefit and protection, don't hesitate to get help. Make sure you can defer a gain, even on the sale of your house, by conferring with an expert.

■ *CAUTION NOTE:*   *The tax implications of real estate ownership should always be gone over with a competent tax attorney.*

Everything, from deducting interest and property taxes to depreciation techniques, installment sales, and tax-free exchanges, needs the help of your accountant to tailor the specific deal. Whether you are buying or selling, your accountant will know how the current tax law pertains specifically to each of these techniques. You can thus get the maximum return from your real estate.

Proper guidance can save you thousands, if not hundreds of thousands, of dollars in taxes. Expert advice is as important in saving your money as the techniques discussed in this chapter.

■ *KEY POINT:*   *Competent tax advice can save you thousands of dollars in taxes.*

In the next chapter we will show you why real estate and its financing are the quickest way to great wealth.

WHY FINANCING IS 14 THE KEY TO BIG PROFITS

MORTGAGES GIVE YOU THE MONEY TO MAKE MONEY

An old adage says you need money to make money. However, as you've read here, you can get started with very little, and sometimes nothing at all. You don't need a fortune as long as you can get a mortgage.

■ *KEY POINT:* *In real estate you can make a lot of money with a little money and patience.*

A mortgage gives you the money to make money. It allows you to buy a property with only a fraction of the total sale price as a down payment. In this way, you can obtain a home or an investment that in a few years will be worth considerably more than what you paid for it.

■ *KEY POINT:* *A mortgage gives you the money to make money.*

A mortgage gives you a considerable advantage over an investor in the stock market who, in most cases, must put up dollar for dollar for a purchase. In buying an average property, you only have to put down one to two dollars in cash for every ten dollars of mortgage.

■ *KEY POINT: In real estate you need less cash to secure a large as-set than in other investments.*

What we have done here is to show you an easy, guaranteed way to get a mortgage in the shortest amount of time—often the same day. We have explained the different mortgages that you can get, various kinds of creative financing from the seller, and, most valuable of all, how to prepare the mortgage proposal. With this proposal, which apprises a lender of the value of the property you wish to buy and your own financial situation, you can best assure your success.

■ *KEY POINT: A mortgage proposal ensures your success in getting a financing commitment within 24 hours.*

MORTGAGES ARE THE KEY TO REAL ESTATE SUCCESS

A mortgage is the key to making money in real estate. It pro-vides you or your tenants with housing or business locations.

A home is often your first investment, and maybe the only one you will ever make. In dollars, it may bring you the greatest profit. Professional investors, in fact, often seek single-family homes, rent them for a short period, three to four years, and then sell them; the profit is as much or more as if they had bought a multifamily apartment building.

■ *KEY POINT: A home is often your first and best investment.*

Your ability to get a mortgage will determine your success in real estate. What you've come to understand here is that it's really not so much the property as the mortgage that's important in buying. For example, in looking for an investment, you could find a fine, six-unit apartment building but, for one reason or another, be unable to finance it with either a bank or a seller for an acceptable interest rate or the right mortgage plan. The property may be great, but if you can't finance it, it's worthless for all parties—you and the lender.

Many factors are at work. For instance, a similar six-family property in a location the bank likes may mean you will get a mortgage. Whether you liked this second property as much as the first one is unimportant. The fact that you can get the mortgage on it by investing a minimal amount of cash means that you can make the deal.

■ *KEY POINT:* *A mortgage enables the average person to buy a property.*

■ *CAUTION NOTE:* *Without financing, a property's value is worthless to you and the lender.*

A mortgage, then, is the key to making money in real estate.

BORROWING YOUR WAY TO RICHES

Borrowed money, in itself, is of questionable value. But the purpose of a mortgage is to secure property. The money is for a constructive cause; it is not frittered away on stereos or new cars.

■ *KEY POINT:* *Borrowed money in the form of a mortgage is for the purpose of buying a substantial asset.*

Borrowing, then, allows you to multiply a small down payment into a huge profit. For example, let's say you buy a house today for $85,000 and the property increases in value a conservative 5% each year. After six years, you decide to sell. The property has increased almost $29,000, to a new value of $114,000. You originally put down $17,000 and got an 80% mortgage of $68,000. While you were paying off this mortgage, the $85,000 property increased $29,000. You have also paid off some principal on the $68,000 loan.

■ *KEY POINT: A mortgage allows you to turn a small amount of cash into a considerable profit.*

You have also had the deduction of mortgage interest, an advantage not available to a renter, who could be paying the same amount of money to rent the same house.

■ *KEY POINT: Mortgage interest deductions give you a tremendous tax advantage over a renter.*

These gains can all be attributed to the mortgage. How often can you make $29,000 on an investment of $17,000, an increase of 74%! And there are many ways, such as a second mortgage or personal loan, to reduce the down payment and thus multiply your profits even more.

■ *KEY POINT: A mortgage is the springboard for all profits in real estate.*

Borrowing money, in the form of a mortgage, on real estate, whether a home or an investment, is your path to riches.

MORTGAGES ARE THE QUICKEST WAY TO GREAT WEALTH

As we've seen, the first step in profiting from real estate is obtaining a mortgage. This is the key to securing property which will grow in value and bring you wealth.

■ *KEY POINT: Getting the mortgage is the key to wealth in real estate.*

If, suddenly, there were no such thing as financing property, the real estate industry would not collapse. We would still need living and business quarters. But it would limit our ability to profit as much. This can be shown by using the last example. Were you to buy that $85,000 house with $85,000 in cash and sell it for $29,000 more, your return would only be 34%—not the 74% you could make in putting down $17,000. The mortgage then, makes a home or an investment a financial bonanza for you.

Real estate is the largest financial asset on which the average person can borrow money in the United States. If you are a big financial wheeler-dealer with sufficient money and expertise you can buy and sell oil wells. With real estate, you don't need any particular know-how to get started.

■ *KEY POINT: Real estate is the largest asset on which the average investor can obtain substantial financing.*

Oil wells are not available to most of us. Getting a mortgage to buy real estate is. In your hometown, there are probably many mortgage banks anxious to lend you money.

■ *KEY POINT: Mortgage money is readily available.*

Real estate mortgages are not some new-fangled way in which to make money. Mortgages have been around almost as long as buildings; they are an age-old way of providing funds.

Some of the great families of America—the Carnegies, Rockefellers, DuPonts—made money from diverse sources as well as real estate. But once they had money, most of it was invested in real estate. Not only did they borrow from the large banks of their day to construct enormous buildings, but they also lent out mortgage money to others.

■ *KEY POINT: The great families of America used real estate to se-cure and maintain their wealth.*

It was Andrew Carnegie who said you could make money in real estate faster than in any other investment. The plethora of books detailing the success stories of self-made millionaires in real estate shows that there is some truth in this.

Real estate is the quickest way to make a fortune, maybe not overnight, but in a reasonable amount of time. With a minimal amount of money and the ability to obtain sizable mortgages, you can make a fortune in little more than a decade.

■ *KEY POINT: You can make considerable money in real estate faster than in any other kind of investment.*

Many books discuss the kinds of property and which to buy. Here we have concentrated on the most important part—getting the mortgage. The key is to get the 80–90% or more of the gross value of your purchase as a loan.

Here you have learned about the different types of mortgages and how to make that all-important presentation to a bank to gain a commitment overnight. The mortgage proposal not only capsulizes the pertinent information needed by the bank to make a decision, but demonstrates that you are competent and you know what you are doing—banks like doing business with professionals.

■ *KEY POINT: Banks respond favorably to a mortgage proposal be-cause your preparation and research show you know what you are doing and care about meeting the bank's needs.*

Even if you buy only one home in your lifetime, the mortgage proposal will make it easier for you to negotiate with the bank. Whether you buy a residence or a million-dollar apartment building, the process is the same.

■ *KEY POINT:* *The proposal demonstrates your professionalism and preparedness.*

NEGOTIATION REQUIRES PREPARATION

Many books on real estate present "short cuts"; like most no-money-down deals, these questionable techniques don't work so well when you try to use them.

There are no shortcuts in real estate, only wise strategy. Any homeowner or investor knows there is quite a bit of work involved in real estate: getting the mortgage commitment itself, finding the right property (no easy task in itself), and then maintaining the investment property.

■ *CAUTION NOTE:* *Most shortcuts don't work.*

Be prepared—know what mortgages are about and how to negotiate them with a bank or seller to help you get the right mortgage from the right source in the quickest amount of time. This way, when you do find the right property, you are ready to provide detailed information on it and to discuss your financial resources.

■ *KEY POINT:* *Know what mortgages are about and what kind is best for you before you negotiate.*

The mortgage proposal is being up front with the lender. Laying everything out in a businesslike manner is the best way to ensure you'll get a rapid mortgage commitment.

■ *KEY POINT:* *Being square with the lender ensures a quick commitment.*

YOU CAN DO IT ALL IN YOUR SPARE TIME

Preparing a mortgage proposal and negotiating mortgage terms does not require an M.B.A., nor is it a full-time activity. Unless you are a professional landlord with many buildings to manage, everything involved with property, from getting the mortgage to finding the property to placing tenants and dealing with upkeep, can be done part-time.

■ *KEY POINT: You can invest in real estate as a part-time activity.*

That's the beauty of investing in real estate. It's not an operational business in the same sense as a hardware or grocery store. It doesn't usually demand day-to-day management.

All ownership takes is concern and common sense; it is basically a managerial task. Specific knowledge can come later.

■ *KEY POINT: Ownership takes common sense and willingness to learn.*

The first steps, the preparation of the mortgage proposal need take no more than a couple of hours. It can be done in an evening, from information you readily have at hand.

THE POWER OF USING OTHER PEOPLE'S MONEY

A mortgage harnesses the power of other people's money. A mortgage from a bank is really the pooled savings of many different, small investors. In contrast, when the seller gives you financing, it is only his money that's involved. Borrowing other people's money is the cornerstone of our economic system.

Funds flow from one person to another in a continual shifting of economic resources.

■ *KEY POINT:* *Borrowing other people's money through mortgages makes our economic system more democratic.*

Imagine if there was no way to borrow money and everything had to be bought with hard cash. First of all, there might not be as much cash around. It takes the lending of money for additional capital to be earned. If we were on an all-cash system, it would make hard goods like real estate and automobiles affordable only to the rich.

■ *CAUTION NOTE:* *If there were no system of borrowing, only the rich could afford large assets like real estate.*

The power of borrowing—using other people's money—is a democratic way in which monies shift from one to another, making money available to all of us who need it.

SMART MORTGAGE FINANCING CAN GIVE YOU AN INCOME FOR LIFE

Much of this information on mortgages and how to obtain them in the shortest amount of time has been to help you get a home or an investment. However, once you get one mortgage, on your home, for example, you may be stimulated to get another. After all, you have passed the key hurdle in real estate. You have proven yourself adept at financing.

In your spare time, you might look around for a second house to rent out or perhaps a two- or three-family building. Get started in a rental property to gain an income.

■ *KEY POINT: After borrowing money for one property, use this
knowledge to borrow for another.*

In the last chapter we talked about how the interest portion
of a mortgage payment, along with property taxes and other
operational expenses, including depreciation, are deductible.
These are amounts you can deduct against the income you receive from the property.

You can pocket tax-deferred money from your tenants each
month just because you have these large deductions.

As we explained, the tax is not eliminated completely, but deferred until a later time when you sell; then you finally pay the
taxes. The advantage is that in five or ten years you will pay today's cost of deferred monies with cheaper dollars.

■ *KEY POINT: Sheltered rental income puts cash in your pocket and
defers taxes until you sell.*

In a small income property, you use financing to earn income. You can vary the terms of the mortgage to determine
how much income you will get. For example, if you choose a
mortgage with a short-term payoff, such as fifteen years, your
monthly interest and principal payments may be high, thereby
using up much of the income you net after operating expenses.
You may do this to build equity in the property more quickly
and to pay less interest overall. For income purposes, however,
it is best to extend the number of years in which your payments
will be made. Your payments are smaller and you can more easily earn an income over and above your expenses.

■ *KEY POINT: A longer-term mortgage allows you to keep more
cash.*

When you pay a mortgage off faster, your goal is to make a
larger profit when you sell. Instead of concentrating on income

along the way, you make it in one big cash pot. One of the benefits of real estate is that by varying the terms of your mortgage you can choose to make more money now or later.

■ *KEY POINT:* *With a shorter-term mortgage, you build equity more quickly, pay less interest, and profit big when you sell.*

HOW TO SPEND THE THOUSANDS OF DOLLARS YOU'VE SAVED BY READING THIS BOOK

If you use the principles in this book to get only one mortgage for one house in your lifetime, you will have saved a considerable amount of money. Just reducing mortgage points through negotiation can save thousands.

A mortgage proposal outlining the feasibility of the property and your financial situation will in itself save thousands by helping you negotiate the best deal.

■ *KEY POINT:* *Using the mortgage proposal to buy only one house will save you thousands of dollars.*

However, if you really want to harness other people's money and grow wealthy, you must get new mortgages repeatedly. Don't just buy your first house. You will probably buy another house as your needs change. On average, you will deal with several banks to negotiate three to five mortgages in your lifetime.

■ *KEY POINT:* *You will probably negotiate several mortgages in your lifetime.*

Think of doing more. Think of securing financial security for retirement. Think of a college fund for your kids obtained on the equity growth in a duplex. Consider buying a second, single-family house to rent out for cash growth in the future.

■ *KEY POINT: A small investment can allow you to reap future rewards—like putting your kids through college.*

The best way for you to invest those thousands of dollars you have saved by reading this book is to multiply them by investing in more real estate. Put the money down on a property to protect your future.

■ *KEY POINT: What you save from negotiating your first mortgage can be used as the down payment for another property.*

When you combine your down payment with an 80% mortgage, you have a one-to-five leverage. With the average mortgage, for every dollar you invest you have four dollars of other people's money going to work for you. In no other part-time endeavor can you make the money you can in real estate. In no other large asset can you, using other people's money, put this money to work for your benefit. Getting a mortgage, then, is a privileged opportunity to choose wisely and properly.

■ *KEY POINT: Only through a mortgage can we put so few dollars to work and make so much.*

INDEX

Accountants:
  in exchanging, 252
  in installment sales, 252
Adjustable balloon mortgage:
  ballooning prior to end of term,
    127
  negotiating of new rate, 127–128
Adjustable rate mortgage (ARM):
  advantages and disadvantages,
    124–125
  converting to fixed rate, 67, 82, 125
  elastic mortgage, 117
  as financing source, 114, 182–183
  flexibility, 37, 81
  gambling on, 65–67, 95–97, 121–
    122
  graduated payment mortgage
    (GPM), 115–116
  growing equity mortgage (GEM),
    118
  index, 82, 113–114, 117, 122
  negotiating, 38, 128–130
  pitfalls, 130–132
  pledged account mortgage (PAM),
    117
  problems with, 96
  and sellers, 43
  shared-appreciation mortgage
    (SAM), 118–120
  and variations, 52, 113, 129
Affordability, 57–68:
  adjusting down payment, 62
  affected by points, 64–65
  in ARMs, 58–59, 66

  borrowing power, 62
  deciding how much, 57–67, 83
  Fannie Mae, 60–61
  loan guidelines, 60–61, 83–84
  and mortgage insurance, 64
  problem of low down payment, 63
  shopping for rate, 58, 70–76
  and variable rate, 65–67
Agents, help from, 54
Agreements to purchase, short form,
  42–43
All-inclusive mortgage, see
  Wraparound
Appraisal:
  bank appraisal, 9
  comparable sales, 14
  general, 7–9
  meeting criteria, 8
  mini-appraisal, 12–14
  verifying value, 8, 13–14
Assumption:
  assumable mortgage, 51
  by buyers, 51, 83, 135–136
  existing mortgage, 104–106
  as financing source, 185–186
  non-assumable clause, 103, 143–
    144
  taking "subject-to," 110, 136, 138
  see also Mortgages

Balloon mortgage, see Adjustable
  balloon mortgage
Balloon payments:
  as financial source, 196–197

Balloon payments (*cont.*)
  in seller's mortgage, 134, 139
  in shared-appreciation mortgage
    (SAM), 119
Banker, see Lender
Bi-weekly mortgage, 197–198
Blanket mortgage, as financial
    source, 195
Bond for deed, 143–144

Capital gains:
  under new law, 234, 238
  sought, 231
Chattel goods, as financial source, 198
Choosing, 69–84:
  adjustable rate, 71–72
  anticipating future income, 69
  comparing loans, 76–83
  fixed rate, 71–72
  higher down payment, 70
  and interest rate, 75–76
  and property costs, 75
  shopping for, 70–72
  six points, 83–84
Closing costs:
  getting seller to pay, 170
  in government financing, 170
  in home equity loan, 204
  in refinancing, 222–225
Commercial banks, as financial
    source, 88, 159
Commercial loans, as financial
    source, 190–191
Contract for deed, as financial
    source, 195
Conventional mortgage:
  affordability, 63, 65–67
  assuming existing, 104–106
  choosing, 71–72, 97–98
  inside tips, 110–112
  limits, 109–110
  and points, 97, 102–103, 110
  and red tape, 103–104
  shopping for, 98–99
  standard loan, 32–35
  and term, 72–73

Cooperative banks, 87
Counselor, help from real estate, 55
Cover letter, 21–22
Creative financing, 44–46
  combined with conventional
    financing, 45
  less down payment, 45
  second mortgage, 45
  see also Seller financing
Credit union, as financial source, 90

Dealer:
  definition, 248
  tax consequence, 248
Deductions:
  bookkeeping, 231, 242–244
  in home equity loan, 206
  for interest, 241–242, 234
  investment property, 262
  operating expense, 232, 233, 235
  in refinancing, 228–229
  standard deduction, 234
  for taxes, 233
Depreciation:
  bookkeeping, 231, 242–244
  cutting income, 242–244, 246
  home, 244
  investment property, 262
  rental of second home, 239–241
Disclosure, financial, 9
Down payment:
  adjusting, 62
  and affordability, 62
  in exchange, 166–167
  higher, 70
  making, 81, 162
  minimizing, 157–175
  negotiating, 100–102
  problems in minimizing, 63, 173–
    174

Elastic mortgage, fixed payment, 117
  see also Adjustable rate mortgage
    (ARM)
Equity:
  building, 262

in exchange, 249
payments in GEM, 118
purchase in foreclosure, 171
refinancing, 194–195
through a reverse mortgage, 177–179
Exchanging:
  as financial source, 190
  of home, 236
  "like-kind," 247–248
  minimizing down payment, 40, 166–167
  in seller financing, 151–152
  tax advisor, 247
  tax deferral, 246–249
  tax free, 246–248
Exclusion, fifty-five or older, 235, 237
Exemption, personal, 234, 238–239

Federal Housing Administration (FHA):
  appraisal, 41
  closing costs, 170
  Fannie Mae, 60–61
  as financial source, 167, 186
  minimum cash down, 40, 167
Financial profile:
  credit, 17
  personal, 14–18
Fixed rate mortgage, see Conventional mortgage

GI loan, see Veterans Administration (VA)
Government loans, see Federal Housing Administration (FHA); Veterans Administration (VA)
Graduated payment mortgage (GPM):
  combined with adjustable rate, 116
  minimal beginning payments, 115
  as type of ARM, 115
  see also Adjustable rate mortgage (ARM)
Growing equity mortgage (GEM):
  as based on growing equity, 118

see also Adjustable rate mortgage (ARM)
Guarantees, 101. See also Federal Housing Administration (FHA); Veterans Administration (VA)
Guidelines, 60–61. See also Mortgage

Home equity loans, 199–214:
  alternative to second mortgage, 200
  bookkeeping, 208
  borrowing limits, 203
  closing costs, 204
  composing basic elements, 201–203
  credit line, 199
  deductibility, 206–208
  gaining cash, 199
  guidelines, 209
  less cost, 199–200
  problems, 210
  repayment schedules, 205
  types, 200–201
Home office, 236

Index, see Adjustable rate mortgage (ARM)
Individual Reverse Mortgage Account (IRMA), 178
Installment sale:
  tax advisor, 252
  tax breaks, 250
  and taxes, 239
Insurance company, as financial source, 90
Interest:
  in adjustable balloon, 127
  adjustable rate, 35, 81
  and affordability, 57
  ARM fluctuation, 110, 114, 117, 122–124
  competition lowers, 107–108, 215
  consumer, 234
  deductibility, 233, 241–242
  fixed rate, 33
  gambling on rate, 95–97
  in home equity loan, 201–203

Interest (*cont.*)
  less interest, 50
  limiting swings, 130
  lower rate, 99, 101, 120, 215, 217
  negotiating, 100, 106–108
  paid in long term, 48
  problems in rate, 112, 114, 119
  and refinancing, 97
  rising protection, 123–124
  in second mortgage, 138
  with seller, 135
  shopping for rate, 57, 75–76
  tax law treatment, 233, 234
  wraparound, 143
Investment property:
  financing, 46–47
  income for life, 261–263
  property values, 155
  similarity with financing home, 139

Land Sales Contract, see Contract for
    deed
Lawyers:
  advice in MAO, 149
  help from, 55, 140, 222
  help in exchange, 152
Lease with option to buy:
  as financial source, 187
  no money down, 166–167
  with seller, 144–147
Lenders:
  contact with, 29, 91–93, 99
  decision made by, 8
  equity, 17
  limits of, 109–110
  profitability, 10, 19–20
  truth, 4
Life estate, as financial source, 192–
    194
Limited partnership, as financial
    source, 191–192
Loan, see Mortgage

Management agreement with option
    (MAO):

as financial source, 187–188
  minimize down payment, 149, 169
  with seller, 148–150
Mini-appraisal, see Appraisal
Mortgage:
  agreement, 31
  ARMs, 35–40
  assumption, 51–52, 104–106, 185–
    186
  bi-weekly, 197–198
  blanket, 195
  choosing, 3, 95–97
  commitment in 24 hours, 1–29
  comparison shopping, 27, 76–83
  conventional, 32–35, 182
  creative, 44–46
  definition, 2, 31
  discounting balance, 219–220
  foreclosure, 2, 4, 17, 32, 171
  gambling on rate, 95–97
  guidelines, 60–62, 80–83
  home equity, 199–213
  home vs. investment, 46–47
  honesty in, 26
  insurance, 64, 168
  negotiating, 19, 153
  non-assumable, 46
  obtaining, 6
  persistence, 27
  points in, 33
  price-level adjusted, 179–181
  and property cost, 75
  proposal, 10–26
  purchase money, 185–186
  refinancing on purchase, 194
  restructuring, 216
  reverse, 177–179
  second, 45, 149, 183
  secret in quick, 28–29
  sources, 85–93
  and success, 254–255
  and taxes, 231–252
  term comparison, 218
  third, 183
  time period, 47–50, 262–263

tips in getting, 110–112
trust deed, 196
trust deed with balloon payment, 196–197
wraparound, 141–143, 190
Mortgage agreement terms, 50–53
Mortgage brokers:
  as financial source, 89
  and points, 89
Mutual savings banks, as financial source, 87–88

Negative amortization, 131. See also Adjustable rate mortgage (ARM)
Negotiating:
  in adjustable balloon mortgage, 127
  ARMs, 123
  with banks, 87, 109
  down payment, 100–102
  financing, 47, 259
  lower interest, 100–102, 106
  manageable payments, 128–130
  no money down, 161
  and points, 103, 110, 131
  preparation, 259
  prepayment penalties, 131
  professional help, 53–55
  releases, 52
  renegotiating, 216–217
  in SAM, 129
  with sellers, 86, 153
  several mortgages, 263–264
  terms, 102–108

One-day loans, 7
Other people's money (OPM), 4, 260–261, 263

Partnership, in buying property, 172–173. See also Limited partnership
Pending sale, 6
Pension funds, as financial source, 90

Personal loans, as financial source, 190–191
Pledged account mortgage (PAM):
graduated payments, 117
  see also Adjustable rate mortgage (ARM)
Points:
  affecting affordability, 64–65
  in conventional loan, 102–103
  extra charge, 33, 50
  government loan, 41
  by mortgage brokers, 89
  negotiating, 110
  origination, 131
  prepayment, 50–51, 82, 131
  refinancing, 97, 221, 230
Prepayment penalty, see Points
Price-level adjusted mortgage (PLAM), 179–181
Professionals:
  help from, 53–55
  lawyers, 55
  real estate agents, 54
  real estate counselors, 55
Property taxes, see Taxes
Proposal:
  cover letter, 21–22
  ensuring profitability, 18–21
  financial profile, 14–18
  general, 10–26
  key to success, 258
  made in spare time, 260
  mini-appraisal, 12–14
  personal contact, 29
  undo red tape, 103–104
  writing, 26
Purchase money mortgage, as financial source, 185. See also Seller financing

Rates, see Interest
Refinancing, 215–230:
  costs of, 221–222
  discounting balance, 219–220
  as financial source, 194

Refinancing (*cont.*)
  guideline, 229
  lower rate, 217–219
  making decision, 222–225
  renegotiating, 216–217, 219
  renegotiating fixed rate, 97
  restructuring, 216
  saving money, 215–216
  second mortgage, 227–228
  source, 226
  term comparison, 218, 219
Renegotiable mortgage, 125–127
  converting to fixed rate, 125
  limiting swings, 126
  see also Adjustable rate mortgage
    (ARM)
Repurchase option, as financial
    source, 197
Reverse mortgage, 177–179

Sale-leaseback, as financial source,
    188–189
Savings banks, as financial source, 87
Second mortgage:
  alternative to, 200
  from builder, 139–140
  creative financing, 45
  as financial source, 183–184
  in management agreement with
    option, 149
  no money down, 158–160, 164
  in refinancing, 227–228
  from seller, 133–134
  see also Mortgage
Seller financing, 133–156
  assuming, 133–137
  bond for deed, 143
  commitment, 24
  convincing, 23–25
  exchange, 151–152
  as financial source, 85–86, 184–185
  financing, 41, 47
  lease with option, 144–147, 168
  letter, 23–25
  management agreement with
    option, 148–150

mortgage, 23
  motivation key to, 153
  mutual advantage, 133–135
  no money down, 158–162, 164
  secondary financing, 138–140
  selling yourself, 153
  wraparound, 141–143
  see also Creative financing
Shared-appreciation mortgage
    (SAM):
  lender shares equity, 118–120
  no money down, 165
  see also Adjustable rate mortgage
    (ARM)
Sources, 85–94:
  of refinancing, 226
  selecting best, 91–93
  from seller, 85
  where to go, 85–93
"Subject to," see Assumptions

Tax basis, 244–246
  in exchange, 249
Taxes:
  advice, 252
  basis, 244–246
  benefit of new law, 231–232
  bookkeeping depreciation, 231,
    235, 242–244
  brackets, 234
  capital gains, 234, 238
  consequences, 83
  deductibility, 233
  deferring, 152, 237, 262
  exchanging, 152, 246–249
  exclusion, one-time, 235, 237
  highlights of, 234–235
  home equity deductibility, 206–208
  home office, 236
  installment sale, 239, 250
  interest treatment, 234, 241–242
  and mortgages, 231
  personal exemption, 234
  rates, 234, 252
  in refinancing, 228–229
  rental of second home, 239–241

on sale, 235, 236
sales tax, 234
shelter, 235
standard deduction, 234
state and local, 234
Techniques, 177–198:
   ARM, 182–183
   assumed mortgage, 185–186
   bi-weekly mortgage, 197–198
   blanket mortgage, 195
   borrow on equity, 194–195
   commercial or personal loan, 190–
      191
   contract for deed, 195–196
   conventional, 182
   exchanging property, 190
   FHA loan, 186
   GI guarantee, 186–187
   lease with option to buy, 187
   life estate, 192–194
   limited partnership, 191–192
   management agreement with
      option to buy (MAO), 187–188
   price-level adjusted mortgage
      (PLAM), 179–181
   purchase money mortgage, 185–
      186
   refinance on purchase, 194
   repurchase option, 197
   reverse mortgage, 177–179
   sale-leaseback, 188–189
   second mortgage, 183–184
   third mortgage, 183–184

trade-in property or chattel goods,
   189
trust deeds, 196
wraparound mortgage, 190
Term, see also Mortgage and
   Negotiating:
   extending life, 82
   negotiating, 107–108
   short or long, 72–75
Third mortgage, as financial source,
   183–184. See also Second
   mortgage
Trade-in property, as financial
   source, 189. See also Exchange
Treasury bill rate, 114
Trust deed, as financial source, 196
Trust deed with balloon payment,
   196–197

Variable rate loan (VRL), see
   Adjustable rate mortgage (ARM)
Veterans Administration (VA):
   appraisal, 41
   closing costs, 170–171
   as financial source, 167, 186–187
   limits, 40
   no down payment, 40, 167

Wraparound:
   creating financing, 45–46
   as financial source, 190
   with seller, 141–143
   see also Mortgage